WORLD WAR II
BATTLE OF RUSSIA

WORLD WAR II
BATTLE OF RUSSIA

Published by Bookmart Ltd 2005

Blaby Road,
Wigson,
Leicester,
LE18 4SE
Books@bookmart.co.uk

All notations of errors or omissions (author inquiries, permissions) concerning the content of this book should be addressed to TAJ Books 27, Ferndown Gardens, Cobham, Surrey, UK, KT11 2BH, info@tajbooks.com.

ISBN 1-84509-170-1

Printed in China.
1 2 3 4 5 08 07 06 05

Contents

THE ARMIES FACE TO FACE   6

BARBAROSSA: THE STORM BREAKS   14

TARGET MOSCOW   20

STALIN HITS BACK   28

RUSSIA HITS BACK   32

DRIVE TO THE CAUCASUS   38

THE RUSSIAN CONVOYS   48

THE LONG AGONY   52

STALINGRAD: THE TRAP CLOSES   58

STALINGRAD AND AFTER   66

KURSK: GREATEST LAND BATTLE   74

SMASHING THE DNIEPR FRONT   82

ASSAULT FROM THE EAST   90

ON TO THE VISTULA   96

THE BATTLE OF LAKE BALATON   104

CHRONOLOGY OF WORLD WAR II   109

Russia's time runs out

Hitler's decision to attack the Soviet Union was made at Berchtesgaden between July 20 and 29, 1940. He was motivated partly by the vulnerability of the indispensable Ploie ti oil fields to Soviet Bombers.

On June 22, 1941, at dawn, 3,400,000 Germans launched a surprise attack on the Soviet Union, defended by the 4,700,000 men of the Red Army, as Russia's army was called. In the numbers engaged and the losses suffered on both sides, this titanic struggle, unprecedented in human history, had no equal in any other theatre of operations in World War II. It would go on until the annihilation of the Wehrmacht, expressed in the smoking ruins of Berlin, and the signing of the instrument of unconditional surrender by Field-Marshal Keitel, followed by Grand-Admiral von Friedeburg and Colonel-General Stumpff of the Luftwaffe, in the presence of Marshal of the U.S.S.R. Georgi Zhukov, General Carl Spaatz of the United States Army Air Force, Air Chief-Marshal Sir Arthur Tedder of the R.A.F., and General de Lattre de Tassigny of France.

It must be stated in introduction that there are many aspects of this tragic struggle which, even today, have not been clarified. There is an abundant German bibliography on the Eastern Front operations, in the form of memoirs, general or specialised histories, monographs and published documents, but nothing of the kind is available on the other side of the Iron Curtain. Historical research, which suffered under Stalin, was also weak in the period of "destalinisation", and the disgrace of Nikita Kruschev was reflected in new instructions as imperious as those of previous epochs.

But does the quality of Soviet historical publication compensate for its lack of quantity? Not in the opinion of Alexander Werth, who was the Sunday Times correspondent in Moscow throughout the war. In the introduction to his book Russia at War he writes:

"… but even the longest of them, the vast six-volume Russian History of the Great Patriotic War of the Soviet Union running to over two million words, and trying to cover not only the military operations, but 'everything', is singularly unsatisfactory in many ways. It contains an immense amount of valuable information which was not available under Stalin; but it is overburdened with names of persons, regiments and divisions and an endless variety of military and economic details. It is full of ever-recurring 'heroic' clichés."

Whatever their differences, all the Soviet authors consulted in German translation are in agreement on one point, or rather one dogma, summarised neatly by Colonel-General P. A. Kurochkin in his conclusion to the collective work entitled The Most Important Operations of the Great Patriotic War:

"The colossal victory of the Soviet armed forces in the Great Patriotic War proves indisputably the progressive nature of Soviet military skill and its incontestable superiority over the military art of bourgeois armies."

This condemnation evidently includes not only the defeated in that merciless war, but also Russia's British and American allies. And as the statement is "indisputable", those who dare to question it prove, by doing so, their incurable ignorance or cynical bad

An Italian motorised until on its way to the front.

faith. Such doubters are anathematised as "bourgeois falsifiers of history".

The Red Army

More than a quarter of a century after the unconditional surrender of the Third Reich, the initial deployment of the Soviet armed forces, as well as their structure and composition, are still much of a mystery. And since the secrecy which surrounds the subject has no relation, in view of the tremendous development of all arms, to present day security, the only conclusion that can be reached is that for reasons of domestic and international politics and propaganda, Moscow wishes to draw a veil over certain aspects of the great struggle.

The result is that, whereas with the aid of documents published in West Germany the German order of battle is known in detail down to divisional and even lower level, the semi-official History of the Great Patriotic War of the Soviet Union describes the Soviet forces, on the day of confrontation, only down to army level.

Between the Arctic and the Black Sea, the Red Army was deployed in five major groups. The Soviet dispositions formed a long, undulating line along the western frontier. The organisation within the Military Districts was poor (with reserve units too far back to give effective support to the front line troops) and there was little real coordination between the Districts.

Although considerable effort had been invested in the construction of field fortifications in strategically vital areas (over 200,000 men were engaged in the task), the results failed to live up to expectations. In what was supposedly an interlocking system of defence, gaps 10 to 80 kilometres wide were apparent.

A further problem facing the Soviet commanders was Stalin's own curious attitude towards the possibility of war. Because of Stalin's refusal to heed the warnings of impending invasion he forbade his generals to mobilise their forces in anticipation of attack. He maintained that any sizeable troop movements would be construed by the Germans as "provocation".

The most serious flaw in the Russian dispositions was their forward deployment which made it quite impossible for the Soviet commanders to react effectively to the swiftness of the German invasion. The reasoning behind the decision to defend the frontier line of the Soviet Union was based on two erroneous assumptions: firstly, that a formal declaration of war would precede offensive operations, so that the Red Army would not be surprised, and secondly, that the enemy offensive would be opened with limited forces, thereby giving the army time to fight holding actions and allow a full mobilisation. The folly of these assumptions would soon be fully exposed.

Russian soldiers loading shells into tank.

If we consider the Red Army in more detail we see that it was quite unprepared for modern war. A fundamental problem acting against military efficiency was the absence of effective communications. Radio equipment was in short supply, especially so in the armoured formations and the air force. Basic communication was carried out through the civilian network so that in one instance, noted by Professor Erickson, the signals of the 22nd Tank Division were sent through a local post-office, the unit "plugging-in" to the civilian network and telegraph service!

Similarly in the fields of transport and supply the Russian armed forces were woefully deficient. The Motorised Transport branch was another victim of administrative ineptitude: its independent status was removed, being reassigned to the armoured forces. However, the armoured units proved incompetent in this additional role.

As Professor Erickson explains, within the Red Army there was a general failure to put theory into practise:

"Throughout the whole of the Soviet military sector, from research and development to tactical training, the pressure was on, but its application was uneven, uncoordinated and in parts uncomprehending."

Soviet naval strength

We have already noted Stalin's desire to build up a strong navy in the chapter on German military aid to Russia. On June 22, 1941, the Soviet Navy possessed no fewer than 139 submarines, distributed thus: Arctic Ocean 14; the Baltic 74; and the Black Sea 51. In other classes of vessel the Russian Navy was weak, having only a few modern cruisers and destroyers, but this submarine fleet was the largest in the world.

Its size was not, however, matched by its successes. Between June 22, 1941 and May 8, 1945, it sank only 292,000 tons of shipping, compared with Germany's 14.5 million tons, the United States' 5.5 million tons, and Great Britain's 1.8 million tons. It is true that the Arctic, Baltic, and Black Sea offered far less in the way of prey than the North Atlantic, Pacific, and Mediterranean, but all the same, not until the end of 1944 were Soviet submarines able to interfere significantly with the seaborne supply or evacuation of German troops, and with imports of Swedish iron ore.

It must be admitted, however, that Germany's main lines of communication lay on land, and thus even had they been more efficient, there would have been little that the submarines could do.

Surprise on the side of the Germans

Such were the strengths and weakness of the Soviet land, sea, and air forces. But the defeats which the Russians suffered in four continuous months, and the German's advance to the suburbs of Moscow, cannot be explained without mentioning the factor of surprise, of which the invaders made full use right from the beginning of the campaign. Naturally, Hitler and O.K.H. had camouflaged as best they could the 153 German divisions which would go into the attack on June 22, and they had also made several diversionary feints.

"For two days," writes Paul Carell, "they had been lying in

the dark pinewoods with their tanks and their vehicles. They had arrived, driving with masked head-lights, during the night of June 19–20. During the day they lay silent. They must not make a sound. At the mere rattle of a hatch cover the troop commanders would have fits. Only when dusk fell were they allowed to go to the stream in the clearing to wash themselves, a troop at a time.

"The regiment was bivouacking in the forest in full battle order. Each tank, moreover, carried ten jerricans of petrol strapped to its turret and had a trailer in tow with a further three drums. These were the preparations for a long journey, not a swift battle. 'You don't go into battle with jerricans on your tank,' the experienced tankmen were saying.

"A fantastic rumour swept through the field kitchens. 'Stalin has leased the Ukraine to Hitler and we're just going to occupy it.'"

Hitler himself had had his command post carefully concealed. "This great H.Q.," recalls Paul Schmidt, "was hidden in a thick forest near Rastenburg in East Prussia. One recalled the old tales of witches. Not without reason was the H.Q. known by the code-name of Wolfsschanze (Wolf's lair).

"The atmosphere of the post in the dark Prussian forest was depressing for people coming from sunnier parts.

"The rooms were tiny. You always felt constricted. The humidity which came from masses of concrete, the permanent electric light, the constant hum of the air-conditioning imposed an air of unreality on the atmosphere in which Hitler, growing paler and more flabby every day, received the foreign visitors. The whole place might easily have been the mystic retreat of some legendary spirit of evil."

Nevertheless, since the coming of spring, London, Vichy, Berne, Stockholm, Tokyo, and Washington had been expecting a decisive split between the signatories of the German-Soviet Non-Aggression Pact of August 23, 1939, and were already calculating the effect this immense extension of the war would have.

Only the Kremlin refused until the last moment to admit that Hitler was about to cross his Rubicon. Stalin took none of the measures which were clearly required if Russia was to be prepared for the imminent change in the political and military situation. The Great Patriotic War explains his strange blindness in this way:

"One of the reasons for the error made in the appreciation of the situation is that J. V. Stalin, who alone decided the most important political and military questions, was of the opinion that Germany would not break the Non-Aggression Pact in the near future. Therefore he considered all the reports of German troop movements merely as evidence of provocations, intended to force the Soviet Union into counter-measures.

"If he took such measures, Stalin feared he might furnish the Hitlerian clique with a good pretext for accusing the U.S.S.R. of having broken the treaty and attacking Germany treacherously. For the same reasons, certain commanders of military districts who wanted to place their troops in defensive positions and have them ready for combat, had their requests refused.

"The People's Defence Commissar, Marshal of the Soviet Union Timoshenko, and G. K. Zhukov, Chief-of-Staff, bear a heavy burden of responsibility for the unpreparedness of the Red Army to resist a surprise attack. They had not appreciated

German tanks advancing into Russia.

the military and political situation clearly enough and had not understood that immediate measures to put the armed forces into combat readiness were essential."

There is nothing surprising in Stalin's refusal to believe Churchill's warning about an imminent German attack. The message that the British Prime Minister sent him on April 3 and which, for various reasons, was not handed him until the 22nd was not explicit enough to have made him change his views:

"Prime Minister to Sir Stafford Cripps [British Ambassador in Moscow] "Following from me to M. Stalin, provided it can be personally delivered by you:

"I have sure information from a trusted agent that when the Germans thought they had got Yugoslavia in the net — that is to say, after March 20 — they began to move three out of the five Panzer divisions from Rumania to southern Poland. The moment they heard of the Serbian revolution this movement was countermanded. Your Excellency will readily appreciate the significance of these facts."

Stalin did nothing, fearing that Churchill, using all kinds of forged information, was trying to create a split between Berlin and Moscow and to divert the weight of German arms from Great Britain to the Soviet Union. Though history has shown these suspicions to be groundless, the man in the Kremlin cannot be blamed for being on his guard.

Soviet spies at work

The fact remains, however, that the British message of April 3 was soon corroborated by a deluge of information which ought to have found more credence in Moscow, since it originated from Soviet spy networks in the Far East and Central Europe.

At the outbreak of war the Frankfurter Zeitung's Far East correspondent, Richard Sorge, long in the pay of the Soviet Secret Service, had been sent as Press Attaché to the German Embassy in Tokyo. General Eugen Ott, Hitler's envoy to the Mikado, was well connected in Japanese circles and kept no secrets from Sorge.

So, on May 19, this informer, an old hand at his calling and particularly well placed, reported the concentration of nine armies (which was correct) and 150 German divisions (he underestimated by three) facing the Soviet frontiers. On June 1, he described the strategy the Nazis would use; and on June 15, he gave June 22 as the date of attack. "Too good to be true," it might have been thought, when the first revelations of Richard Sorge's exploits appeared some 20 years ago. The fact that in 1964 the Kremlin awarded him posthumously the title of "Hero of the Soviet Union" and issued a commemorative postage stamp, indicates the importance of his services to Russia.

In Switzerland there was a network known to the Abwehr as the "Red Trio" (or "Lucy Ring") because of the three clandestine transmitters which it used to communicate from Lausanne and Geneva.

The three "musicians", as they were known in Moscow, were led by the German Rudolf Rössler, known under the codename "Lucy", a German refugee of Christian Progressive hue who lived, ostensibly, as a bookseller in Lucerne. Where did this agent obtain the information that he communicated to Moscow? Even today this question is difficult to answer. From the value of the information he gathered and the three or four days he took to obtain it each time, it is reasonable to conclude that he got it from someone who took part in the most secret conferences of O.K.W.

A proof of this, in respect of Operation "Barbarossa", is the description of Rössler's information given by General Otto Heilbrunn in the book he wrote about the Soviet Secret Service. "Not only had the 'Red Trio' given the date of the attack to its Moscow control, but it had also supplied the German plan of campaign, the composition and numbers of Army Groups "North", "Centre", and "South", with precise details of the number of tanks and their distribution between the groups. What is more, Moscow now knew the intentions of the enemy, his directions of attack, and his precise objectives. Lastly Moscow was told the names of all senior officers down to the corps commanders."

Never had a state been better informed than Russia about the aggressive intent of another. Never had the accuracy of the information been so highly guaranteed, since there could have been no collusion between Sorge and Rössler. But never had an army been so ill-prepared to meet the initial onslaught of its enemy than the Red Army on June 22, 1941.

With 138 infantry divisions and 40 motorised and armoured divisions under arms between the frozen Arctic Ocean and the Danube delta, the Red Army could have been expected to hold the attack of some 200 German and satellite divisions, had it been properly deployed for a defensive campaign. But it was not. The troops of the Baltic Special Military District were dispersed between the Niemen and the Dvina to a depth of nearly 200 miles. It was worse in the West Special Military District where General Pavlov had placed divisions along the whole 300 mile line between Bialystok and Minsk.

This dispersal of Soviet Forces was the pattern the length of the German-Russian demarcation line. There is no getting away from the fact that the fronts were too long for the divisions detailed to garrison them. For instance, according to the Great Patriotic War, the Russians had only the 125th Division covering a 25-mile front facing Panzergruppe IV which, on June 22, put two infantry divisions and three armoured divisions into the field. The situation was the same in the sectors awaiting the onslaught of Hoth and Guderian, powerfully supported by Colonel-General von Richthofen's Stukas.

On June 18, a German deserter crossed into the Russian lines near Kovel' and reported the attack as coming on June 22.

But this extra proof provoked no greater reaction from the Kremlin than the information it had previously received. Nevertheless, on the night of June 21, after midnight, the penny dropped and at 0030 hours the commanders of the military districts concerned were ordered to occupy their front line positions, disperse and camouflage their aircraft, and put the A.A. on full alert. But they were not to take "any other steps without special orders". This instruction, however, insufficient as it was, had not reached all commanders before they found themselves at grips with forces which were very much greater in numbers and in armament. Furthermore, the Russian communications with the rear had been cut by the German artillery bombardment, which began at 0335 hours that morning and destroyed the Russian telephone networks. At 0415 the barrage of shells was followed by the wide-ranging destruction of Russian barbed wire by German sappers. The Stukas, diving from high in the sky, alternated with the artillery in pounding the bewildered Soviet Union.

Aftermath of intensive hand-to-hand fighting.

On the evening of June 22, in the headquarters which German G.H.Q. had just taken over at Lötzen in East Prussia, Halder observed in his invaluable diary:

"The enemy has been taken unawares by our attack. His forces were not tactically in position for defence. In the frontier zone his troops were widely dispersed and his frontier defence was weak overall.

"Because of our tactical surprise, enemy resistance on the frontier has been weak and disorganised. We have been able to seize bridges over the border rivers and, slightly further on, to overwhelm enemy positions fortified by deep earthworks."

Stalin's failure to react until the very eve of the German attack is astonishing. Some validity can be given to the explanation given by one of the best-informed biographers of the Russian leader:

"At dawn on June 22, 1941," writes Emmanuel d'Astier de la Vigerie, "on the day before the anniversary of Napoleon's crossing of the Niemen, 120 divisions speed towards Kiev, Leningrad, and Moscow, where the theatre is performing A Midsummer Night's Dream.

"Stalin, living in a dream world of hope, has spurned warnings and refused advice. During the first hours of the attack he issued orders that German firing is not to be answered. He would like to think he is faced by nothing more than a provocative act from a few ill-disciplined German units. On June 21, a German

Russian village set alight by German troops during the scorched earth policy.

Communist worker deserted and revealed the date and time of the attack. Stalin is told but refuses to believe the evidence. Fifteen years later Nikita Khruschev recounts the episode; and another historian adds that Stalin ordered Korpik, the deserting worker, who could in his view only be an agent provocateur, to be shot."

Soviet resistance in chaos

To the north of the Pripet Marshes, Soviet resistance had, from the early hours of that warm summer morning, been surprised and overcome more or less everywhere. The same fate had overcome reinforcements moving up to the front to obey People's Defence Commissar Marshal Timoshenko's broadcast message of 0715 hours

"Our troops must hurl themselves with all their means and energy against the enemy and annihilate them in all places where they have violated our frontiers."

In Army Group "Centre's" area, Colonel-General Guderian had taken the bridges over the River Bug, above and below Brest-Litovsk, by storm, and by the evening his XXIV Panzer Corps (General Geyr von Schweppenburg) was in Kobrin and his XLVII Panzer Corps (General Lemelsen) in Pruzhany, 41 and 47 miles respectively from their jump-off points.

This enormous success by Panzergruppe II was equalled and even surpassed by that of Panzergruppe III. Not only had Colonel-General Hoth penetrated deeply into the Russian defences but his LVII Panzer Corps (General Kuntzen) and his XXXIX Panzer Corps (General R. Schmidt) had taken the bridges over the Niemen at Merkine and Olyta intact. The XXXIX Corps

was in fact 59 miles over the demarcation line.

This ultra-rapid war of movement led at times to comic incidents such as this adventure of General Guderian:

"I next visited the front line in Slonim and then drove in a Panzer IV through no-man's-land to the 18th Panzer Division. At 15.30 hrs I was back in Slonim having ordered the 18th Panzer Division to push on in the direction of Baranovichi, while the 29th (Motorised) Infantry Division was instructed to hasten its advance towards Slonim. I then returned to my Group command post. This drive took me unexpectedly through the middle of Russian infantry, which had come up in lorries to the very outskirts of Slonim and was on the point of dismounting. I ordered my driver, who was next to me, to go full speed ahead and we drove straight through the Russians; they were so surprised by this unexpected encounter that they did not even have time to fire their guns. All the same they must have recognised me because the Russian press later announced my death; I felt bound to inform them of their mistake by means of the German wireless."

In Army Group "North", Field-Marshal von Leeb had no reason to be any less satisfied with the results of the first day of the campaign. Panzergruppe IV (Colonel-General Hoeppner) had also thrown the Russians into disorder; in particular, at about 1900 hours, the LVI Panzer Corps (General von Manstein) had boldly seized the important viaduct which crosses the Doubissa gorges at Airogala. He was about 50 miles from his starting point.

As for the Soviet Air Force, those planes which had not been destroyed on the ground in the first hour made a rather pitiful impression on General Kesselring:

"From the second day onward I watched the battle against the aircraft which were arriving from the depths of Russia. It seemed almost criminal to me that they should use formations which were so ridiculous from the point of view of aerial tactics, and machines obviously incapable) of getting out of trouble in the air. In they came, one squadron after the other, at regular intervals, and one after the other they crashed, easy prey to our fighters. 'This is the massacre of the innocents,' I thought. So completely did we manage to crush the basis of any future bomber fleet that Russian bombers never appeared again throughout the whole campaign!"

In contrast, south of the Pripet Marshes, the achievements of Field-Marshal von Rundstedt had been no greater than what German military theorists call an "ordinary victory", and it had not been possible to split off units from Panzergruppe I (Colonel-General von Kleist) to exploit the success.

The designs of the Third Reich on the Ukraine were known to all and so Stalin had emphasised the defence of the approaches to that territory. It was defended by 68 divisions, including ten armoured and five motorised, while Rundstedt had only 54 divisions under him, including 12 Rumanian, five Panzer, and three motorised divisions. Furthermore, following an order from Hitler, the German 11th Army (seven divisions), which had been concentrated in Moldavia, did not join battle on June 22. This allowed the Russians to assemble part of the forces they had aligned along the Rumanian frontier and use them profitably in Galicia.

The Germans reach the Black Sea

Operation "Barbarossa" had begun very successfully for the Germans, and in the days following June 22 their offensive movements developed at frightening speed, to the disadvantage and dismay of the Russians.

From the Black Sea to the Pripet Marshes, Army Group "South" had finally overcome Soviet resistance. L'vov fell on June 30 and on July 2, the German 11th Army, which included the Rumanian 3rd Army (General Dumitrescu), went over to the attack. Three days later, the German 6th Army (Field-Marshal von Reichenau) succeeded in punching a hole through the fortified positions constructed by the Russians near the old Polish-Soviet frontier; Panzergruppe I drove into the breach along the Berdichev-Zhitomir line and it is possible that its III Panzer Corps (General von Mackensen) would have taken Kiev and the Dniepr bridges if a sudden order from Hitler had not forbidden him to risk his tanks in the city.

He was forced to wait outside Kiev to be replaced by the German 6th Army, and then wheel from the east to the south-east. On August 2, near Pervomaysk, on the Bug, the 6th Army linked forces with Colonel-General von Stülpnagel's 17th Army, which had arrived after forced marches from Vinnitsa.

The Soviet 6th, 12th, and part of the 18th Armies had their lines of retreat cut off and were wiped out. The victors captured 103,000 prisoners, 317 tanks, and 858 guns, all that remained of seven corps (22 divisions). Rapidly exploiting their success, the Germans reached the Black Sea near Ochakov.

Soviet prisoners-of-war marching into captivity.

Army Group "Centre" takes 328,000 prisoners

This success was notable but not as remarkable as that of Field-Marshal von Bock. By June 25, Guderian had arrived at Baranovichi and Hoth had reached Lida and Molodechno, both more than 125 miles east of Bialystok, where the unfortunate Pavlov was still bottled up. On the next day the two Gruppen established first contact at Slonim, and at Minsk on the 29th the pincers closed behind the Russians, who had left the decision to retreat until too late. On July 8, according to Halder's diary, of the 43 divisions in the Soviet 3rd, 4th, 10th Armies, 32 could be taken as annihilated. The Germans counted close on 290,000 prisoners, as well as 2,585 tanks, 1,449 guns, and 246 aircraft captured or destroyed.

A second pincer movement was closed at Smolensk on July 16, when Panzergruppe II, which had advanced to Elnia after forcing the bridges over the Berezina and the Dniepr, met Panzergruppe III, which had sped from Polotsk to Vitebsk and then wheeled south to meet Guderian. Here O.K.H. amalgamated the two Gruppen as the 4th Panzerarmee (Tank Army), with Kluge as its commander.

Unfortunately, Kluge could not get on with his impetuous subordinates, who accused him of failing to understand the tactical possibilities of tanks and restricting their initiative to an intolerable degree. Whatever the effect of this friction, the Smolensk sector was the centre of a huge struggle 'til August 8.

German troops attack Soviet position.

The Russians trapped in the pocket tried to break through the perimeter which hemmed them in. From outside, Timoshenko and Lieutenant-General A. I. Eremenko tried to break through to the besieged Russian forces.

In the final analysis, all was in vain. Marshal Timoshenko was defeated at Roslavl' and Guderian took 38,000 prisoners, 300 tanks, and 300 guns. When fighting ceased in the "cauldron" of Smolensk, a communiqué from O.K.H. announced the capture of 310,000 prisoners and the capture or destruction of more than 3,000 armoured vehicles and 3,000 pieces of artillery. At Elnia, the Panzers were 200 miles from Moscow but, since June 22, they had travelled 440 miles, mostly on unmetalled roads, in dust which had scored their pistons and cylinders mercilessly.

The Gulf of Riga occupied

In Army Group "North", Panzergruppe IV was counter-attacked strongly near Raseiniai on June 24 by the Soviet XII Armoured Corps, which launched 100 immense KV-1 tanks against the Germans. Even so, the Russians were cut to pieces and this success allowed LVI Panzer Corps to take Daugav'pils during the course of 26th without the Russians having time to destroy the bridges over the Dvina. Kaunas and Vilnyus fell to the 16th Army, Liep ja and Riga to the 18th. The Lithuanians and Letts welcomed the Germans as liberators, but Hitler had no intention of restoring their independence.

Beginning his push on July 2, Hoeppner reassembled his Panzergruppe on the right bank of the Dvina, moved up to the fortified Russo-Latvian frontier and forced it at Ostrov, opening the way for his XLI Panzer Corps (General Reinhardt) to capture the important centre of Pskov on the eastern shore of Lake Peipus on July 8, and his comrade Manstein to manoeuvre in the direction of Novgorod. Meanwhile, the 16th Army had established links with the 9th Army (Army Group "Centre") near Vitebsk and the 18th had established itself along a line from Lake Peipus, through Dorpat, to Pärnu on the Gulf of Riga.

From now on, the operations of Army Group "North" would slow down markedly, because of Soviet resistance and counter-attacks and also as a result of the swampy nature of the area and the heavy rain. Another reason was that Leeb had given different objectives to his Panzergruppe IV. Its LVI Panzer Corps was to drive on Novgorod while its XLI Panzer Corps moved towards Narva.

German troops during 1st Russian winter.

Eastern front women volunteers in Moscow.

Planned for September 15, Operation "Typhoon", the attack on Moscow, was delayed until October 2. Army Group "Centre" was reinforced to the strength of 78 divisions, with 14 armoured and eight motorised divisions over and above the 19 and 11 of these units which it already possessed. These units were by now quite depleted and the Panzers had less than half the regulation number of tracked vehicles; the Army group however, was expected to wipe out the Bryansk Front (General Eremenko) and the West Front (General Konev), which contained, according to German information, 14 armies with 77 divisions, of which six were armoured and six cavalry.

The manoeuvre included a double pincer movement.

Panzergruppe II and the 2nd Army formed the southern pincer. The 4th and 9th Armies, which included Panzergruppen III and IV, formed the northern claw. Luftflotten I and II, reinforced with all of Richthofen's Stukas, would support this attack, as a result of which Moscow would fall to the Germans.

Emerging from the area of Glukhov, Guderian swept aside everything in his path. He sped through the gap made on October 1, and his XXIV Panzer Corps drove 90 miles north in two days to take Orel. This achievement allowed the XLVII Panzer Corps, which followed Guderian, to veer north-west, take Bryansk from the rear and link up with the 2nd Army, which had forced the Russian positions along the Desna. In this way, two encircling pockets were formed on either side of the city. Both had surrendered by October 25th.

On the first day of Operation "Typhoon", the 4th Army and Panzergruppe IV concentrated near Roslavl', attacked the left wing of Konev's army and soon made a breakthrough. On the next day Colonel-General Hoeppner began to advance north-east to exploit his success. On October 7, his XL Motorised Corps (General Stumme) entered the city of Vyaz'ma to meet the spearhead of LVI Panzer Corps, which had come under the command of General Schaal as a result of General von Manstein's promotion. To the left of Army Group "Centre", the joint 9th Army and Panzergruppe III poured out of the zone north of Smolensk and easily pierced the right of the Russian West Front. So Colonel-General Hoth was immediately able to unleash his tanks, which reached Vyaz'ma by the date mentioned, after cutting round through Kholm. According to the Germans, the Bryansk and Vyaz'ma pockets yielded 663,000 prisoners from 67 infantry divisions, six cavalry divisions, and various armoured units, as well as 1,242 tanks and 5,412 guns. As usual, Soviet historians contest these figures and Marshal A. I. Eremenko does so in terms which are particularly insulting ("pure and simple lies") to the memory of Colonel-General Guderian, his direct adversary in those tragic October days.

It is only fair to admit that Eremenko's 50th Army was not totally annihilated in the pocket which had been formed to the north of Bryansk. Yet the truth is that, in order to regroup and cause some trouble to the 2nd Panzerarmee (ex Panzergruppe II) near Epifan on November 21, it had had to retreat 170 miles.

The 4th Army exploited the situation even more successfully.

Leaving Roslavl' on October 2, three weeks later Kluge found himself outside Naro-Fominsk, nearly 200 miles from his starting point. So, without claiming absolute reliability for the German figures quoted above, it may safely be concluded that the Red Army had undergone a defeat of incalculable magnitude as a result of "Typhoon."

Rain and mud check the German offensive

Two circumstances came to the aid of the defenders of Moscow.

The quite magnificent weather which favoured the offensive at dawn on October 2 was followed, a few days later, by a long period of rain, sometimes mixed with snow. From October 20 onward, the German armies were literally wading in the mud of the steppes which, in Poland at the end of December 1806, Napoleon had described as the "fifth element". Off the roads, the terrain was generally impassable and, with rare exceptions, the roads themselves were dreadful sloughs where vehicles were seen to disappear completely. All the rivers were in flood, which made it a long and difficult operation to repair the countless bridges that the Russians had destroyed in their retreat. Under these conditions, the motorised supply columns were able to cover only 20 miles a day, or even less. The German units had to be amalgamated more and more frequently because of their losses. At the end of October, outside Kalinin, the 36th Motorised Division of Panzergruppe III had only one quarter of its regulation reserve of ammunition and the 6th Panzer Division had lost all its tractors. In the 2nd Panzerarmee, mud and the wear resulting from the

Ukraine offensive combined to produce an even worse situation. On November 14, by grouping together all the tanks of XXIV Panzer Corps which were still functioning, General Guderian was able to improvise a "brigade" of only 50 machines, yet on June 22, 1941, the 3rd and 4th Panzer Divisions, which formed the XXIV Corps, must have totalled 350 tanks. Taken as a whole, the Panzers had lost the use of about half their effectives. In spite of this, Army Group "Centre" had taken the towns of Kaluga, Mozhaysk, and Rzhev and, by the end of October, it was fighting along the line Yelets–Tula–Naro–Fominsk–Volokolamsk–Kalinin.

Soviet historians of World War II have always rejected unanimously the view that mud played any part in the final check of the German attack on Moscow. It cannot be denied that the massing of brigades of T-34 tanks at the front slowed down the Panzer advance but, on the other hand, there is abundant photographic evidence to illustrate this phase of the campaign and this shows mud up to the hubs of German vehicles, up to the bellies of their horses, and over the knees of their soldiers. This speaks for itself.

Alexander Werth's opinion is more balanced but, despite the distinction of this author, it cannot be advanced as true. Quoting Guderian's recollections, he writes:

"Guderian's argument that rain and mud interfered with the success of the first German offensive against Moscow seems futile, since it affected the Russians as much as the Germans."

This argument seems to ignore the fact that the Russians had all the resources of their railway network, while their adversaries were at a great disadvantage since the Soviets had carried out wide-scale demolitions and evacuated their rolling-stock. Furthermore, the bridges behind them were intact and they could draw supplies from depôts in the rear as they moved back. The pursuing Germans, on the other hand, were getting further from their logistic bases every day. Finally, as Kesselring remarks, in that season of torrential rain, the Luftwaffe was able to fly very few missions in support of the ground troops. Because of their losses, the Russians were in the same position.

Hitler's new offensive plans

Since the beginning of November, Hitler had been forced to recognise that the final objectives of Operation "Barbarossa" would not be achieved by the end of the year. He was thus compelled to fall back on a far more modest programme. According to the new plan:

1. Rundstedt would take Sevastopol' and Rostov, throw his armour across the Don, and conquer Maykop and the Kuban' oil areas;

2. Bock would bring about the fall of Moscow by a pincer attack; and

3. Leeb would push east as far as Tikhvin, then wheel north and link up with the Finns on the Svir'; this would solve the problem of Leningrad.

The final objectives of the original plan had been to reach the Volga between Astrakhan and Gor'ky, and the Northern Dvina between Kotlas and Archangel, but this goal now became the target of a new attack to be launched in 1942 as soon as weather permitted. In spite of the delay, Hitler still felt optimistic.

Parade in Red Square to mark the anniversery of the October Revolution.

Though the enemy had not been literally annihilated, he had been decisively defeated. Hitler's optimism was misplaced. Although the Red Army had suffered a blow of staggering proportions, sustaining heavier numerical losses in six months than any other army in history, it was not finished. Stalin's ruthless control of the Soviet war effort and the fighting spirit of the Red Army had enabled Russia to survive the German onslaught.

The plans were now prepared for the offensive against Moscow, to be carried out by Army Group 'Centre' under von Bock.

In the fulfilment of its task, Army Group "Centre" put six armies into the field:

1. Covered on the right by the 2nd Army, the 2nd Panzerarmee would push north along the Tula-Kolomna line;

2. In the centre, the 4th Army would attack the Russians directly opposite in order to hold them and prevent them escaping encirclement; and

3. Covered on their left by the 9th Army, Panzergruppen IV and III would force a passage over the canal connecting Moscow with the Volga. Then turning south-east, they would meet Guderian as he fanned out from Kolomna.

Though he did not issue his generals with a peremptory order, the Führer's aim was to see his armies solidly installed along a line running from Ryazan', through Vladimir and Yaroslavl', to Rybinsk from where, with the spring, they would move towards

Russian troops fighting German troops in Moscow.

Gor'ky, the ancient city previously known as Nizhny-Novgorod.

In carrying out his task, Bock displayed energy that Keitel describes in his diary as "incredible". The fact remains, nevertheless, that by December 5, 1941, his army group had reached, in the words of the famous military theoretician Karl von Clausewitz, its "limit of strategic consumption". Any fresh movement forward was out of the question, as much because of the exhaustion of the troops as through the obstinate resistance of the Russians.

Russian revenge

Unable to take the great industrial city of Tula, the 2nd Panzerarmee had tried to bring it to its knees by cutting it off, but the Germans had spread themselves over a front of 200 miles. In the centre, the 4th Army had been held up at Zvenigorod. The 2nd Panzer Division of Panzergruppe IV had reached Krasnaya Polyana, 22 miles from Red Square but, on December 4, a young artillery officer in the 2nd Motorised Division Das Reich, belonging to the Waffen-S.S., wrote to his mother:

"These Russians seem to have an inexhaustible supply of men. Here they unload fresh troops from Siberia every day; they bring up fresh guns and lay mines all over the place. On the 30th we made our last attack — a hill known to us as Pear Hill, and a village called Lenino. With artillery and mortar support we managed to take all of the hill and half of the village. But at night we had to give it all up again in order to defend ourselves more effectively against the continuous Russian counter-attacks. We only needed another eight miles to get the capital within gun range — but we just could not make it."

The view of this junior officer is in accord with that expressed by Colonel-General Guderian, who wrote to his wife on November 9:

"We have seriously underestimated the Russians, the extent of the country and the treachery of the climate. This is the revenge of reality."

A last effort by the 7th Panzer Division, once Rommel's division and now part of the Panzergruppe III, under the command of General Reinhardt since the end of October, brought it not only up to the Moscow — Volga canal, but also across it near Dmitrov. A vigorous counter-attack threw it back to the west bank and Reinhardt did not try to regain the lost ground. Besides, with the reversal of fortune, he and his comrade Hoeppner were in a dangerously exposed position and liable to possible flanking attacks.

During the Stalin epoch, Communist sources claimed that this last offensive by Army Group "Centre" had cost it more than 55,000 dead between November 16 and December 6. However the statistics of O.K.H., preserved in Halder's diary, quote losses from November 16 to December 10 as less than 66,000 officers, N.C.O.s and men for the whole of the Eastern Front, and of these only 15,435 were killed or missing. It is true that these losses

threw a terrible burden on the already seriously undermanned German units. For example, in the 7th Division, the infantry regiments consisted of about 400 men each by the end of November, and were commanded by lieutenants.

Georgi Zhukov, born in 1896, made his reputation as a military commander by defeating the Japanese 6th Army in Mongolia in 1939. When Germany attacked in 1941 he served with distinction at Smolensk. On September 11 he replaced Voroshilov in the North and conducted the defence of Leningrad. On October 10 he was appointed C.-in-C. of the West Front. He held the front against two German autumn offensives, and on December 6, 1941 directed the Russian counter-offensive. His next great battle was at Stalingrad, where in mid-November 1942 the Russians trapped the 6th Army.

The Russians attack on the Moscow front

Whatever its mental anguish after the catastrophes of Bryansk and Vyaz'ma, the Soviet High Command had not given up the idea of taking the offensive. During October and November, no less than nine armies, totalling about 50 divisions, were being organised in the rear. On December 1, the Russians estimated that they had reached numerical par with their adversary. Though the Germans were still better equipped with armoured vehicles, they had nothing capable of emerging successfully from a clash with the redoubtable T-34 and KV-1 tanks. This is illustrated by an episode recounted by Colonel Pavel Guds, then a lieutenant and tank commander:

"Our target was a base outside Volokolamsk. The battalion

commander ordered me to support the infantry attack with fire from my KV-1 tank. When our infantry were some way forward, the enemy unleashed a counter-attack, spearheaded by 18 tanks. Our men stopped, wavered, and broke in disorder. They needed help. I ordered my driver to move forward towards the German tanks and my gunner to open fire. Methodically, the Soviet tank destroyed its opponents one after the other. A few minutes later, ten mutilated and burning German tanks lay on the battlefield and the eight survivors were fleeing. On the same occasion, our machines rolled several anti-tank guns flat into the ground.

"When we had finished, we inspected our tank. It bore the marks of 29 impacts and yet it was in first-class condition."

It was also evident that the defenders of Moscow, and the reserves which came flowing in to reinforce them, were perfectly equipped to face the rigours of the climate. A few examples suffice for illustration of this point. The factories of Moscow alone delivered 326,700 pairs of Russian-style boots and 264,400 pairs of fur gloves. The only shortage was in transport, for the 8,000 lorries that the Russians possessed were not sufficient to supply the needs of the attack. The lack was made good by using long columns of trailers and sledges.

The troops who launched the attack on the Germans on December 5 and 6 seem to have had excellent morale. On November 7, the twenty-fourth anniversary of the November Revolution, Stalin had appealed to the patriotic glory of ancient Mother Russia. One after the other he rolled off the names of Alexander Nevsky, who defied the German knights on the frozen Lake Peipus in 1242, Dmitri Donskoy, who crushed the Tartars at Kulikovo in 1380, Minin the Butcher and Pozharsky the Boyar, who raised Moscow against the Poles in 1612, Alexander Suvorov, conqueror of Ismail, Warsaw, and Cassano, and of Mikhail Kutusov, who forced Bonaparte, the victor of Europe, to begin his retreat from Moscow in 1812.

The Soviet offensive on the Moscow front was part of a pattern of movement which aimed at destroying the three German army groups fighting between Lake Ladoga and the Kerch' Strait, which separates the Crimea from Kuban'. For the sake of clarity, and because of its great importance, the great battle which began on December 5 and 6, 1941, will be described first. It began, according to High Command orders, on the immense, 500-mile front which twisted and turned from Kalinin to Yefremov.

Bock's order of battle has already been described and had not been changed to any great extent since about November 15, so there is no need to outline it again.

The thin grey line

However, on account of the considerable losses suffered by the German infantry, the line was thinly held and nowhere were there sufficient troops to cover the front adequately. Army Group "Centre" had spent all its reserves and was by now, to use the expression applied by General Laffargue to the deployment that General Gamelin had tried to organise on May 10, 1940, in a state of "prerupture". Furthermore, the Germans, abandoning their attack on December 4, had only 24 or, at most, 48 hours, according to the sector, to carry out a defensive reorganisation of their newly-won positions. If this were not enough, a temperature

Platoon of German troops moves through a town on their way towards Moscow.

of 34 degrees below zero made the ground so hard that no real fortification work was possible.

This last observation draws attention to the fact that the success of the first Soviet winter offensive can be partially explained by the speed with which the Red Army was able to put its plans into effect. On November 30, Stalin and Shaposhnikov approved the plans drawn up by Zhukov, nicknamed "vinegar-face" or "cropped-head". The plans' first effects became apparent less than one week later.

According to John Erickson in his book The Road to Stalingrad, Konev's Kalinin Front comprised 15 rifle divisions, one motorised rifle brigade, two tank battalions and one cavalry division; Zhukov's West Front 48 rifle divisions (plus three forming in the rear), three motorised rifle divisions, three tank divisions (two without tanks), 15 cavalry divisions, 18 rifle brigades, 15 tank brigades and a parachute corps; Timoshenko's South-West Front (right wing) 11 rifle divisions, one motorised rifle division, six cavalry divisions, one rifle brigade, two tank brigades and a motor-cycle regiment; a grand total of 718,000 men, 7,985 guns and 720 tanks. The Soviet Army's main advantage lay not in numbers, but in fresh, well-clad troops where the Germans were exhausted, ill-fed, demoralised and freezing.

Russia-Red Army fights back.

Like Operation "Typhoon" of October 2, 1941, the Soviet attack launched on December 5 consisted of two pincers designed to crush the flanks of Army Group "Centre". When this result had been achieved, Bock's army group, trapped in front by holding attacks, would be cut off from its communications with Smolensk, surrounded, and annihilated.

To the north-west of Moscow, the salient bounded by the Zvenigorod–Krasnaya–Polyana–Dmitrov–Kalinin line, against which the last efforts of Panzergruppen IV and III and the German 9th Army had spent themselves, would undergo the concentrated assault of the 5th, 16th, and 20th Armies, the 1st Shock Army and the 30th Army of the Moscow Front, as well

as the 31st and 29th Armies of the Kalinin Front, under the command of Generals L. A. Govorov, K. K. Rokossovsky, A. A. Vlasov, V. I. Kuznetsov, D. D. Lelyushenko, I. I. Maslennikov, and Y. Yushkevich respectively.

On the southern side, the forces in the 200-mile salient pushed through the Soviet line by the 2nd Panzerarmee, bordered by Tula, Kashira, Mikhaylov, and Yefremov, would be cut off from their base and crushed by the concentrated attacks of the 50th and 10th Armies (Generals I. V. Boldin and F. I. Golikov), of the Guard Cavalry Corps and the 13th Army (General Gorodnyansky), the latter forming the right wing of the South-West Front.

The Germans were surprised as much by their adversary's initiative as by the vigour and scale of its execution. In effect, by nightfall on D-Day, December 6, General Lelyushenko had penetrated 12 miles into the depleted lines of Panzergruppe III and, on the 11th, a special Kremlin communiqué was able to give details of 400 villages liberated around Moscow, including the small towns of Yakhroma, Solnechnogorsk, and Istra, and the defeat of 17 German divisions, seven of which were armoured and three motorised.

The Volga was secured and would no longer hinder General Konev's forces. In spite of this advantage, they were less fortunate than those of the West Front in their attacks against the German 9th Army. Not till December 16 did they manage to retake Kalinin and fan out south-west. As a result the pincer did not grip the left wing of the German Army Group "Centre", as Moscow had hoped. But, though Hoeppner, Hoth, and Strauss managed to elude the encirclement that threatened them, they did so at the price of losing a large part of their equipment.

Manstein overruns the Crimea

On September 12, Colonel-General von Schobert, commanding the 11th Army, was killed when his aircraft landed in a minefield, and Manstein was appointed to succeed him. The first exploit of the new commander, using the 1st Panzerarmee and the Rumanian 3rd Army, was to annihilate the Russian 18th Army (Lieutenant-General Smirnov); a pocket was created between Bol'shoy-Tokmak and Berdyansk on October 10. In it were trapped 100,000 men, 212 tanks, and 672 guns. Then the German 11th Army turned its attention to the strong position of the Perekop Isthmus which joins the Crimea to the Russian land mass and, on October 29, with the aid of the Stukas, battered the Russian 51st Army (Colonel-General F. I. Kuznetsov). Though he possessed no tanks, Manstein still conducted the Crimean campaign at Blitzkrieg pace. On November 16, his XLII Corps (General von Sponeck) was overlooking the Kerch' Strait and the bulk of the 11th Army was besieging Sevastopol', right at the south of the Crimea.

The Russians parry

The Russian High Command in Moscow now tried to use the situation to its best advantage. While the South Front (General Cherevichenko) took Rostov and pursued the invader back to the Dniepr, the Transcaucasus Front (General Kozlov) would send two armies into the Crimea, lift the siege of Sevastopol' and, crossing the Perekop Isthmus, spread out and harry the retreating

Germans. On November 30, the 9th Army (General Kharitonov), the 17th Army (General Lopatin), and the 18th Army (General Kolpakchy), totalling 22 infantry divisions, nine cavalry divisions, and six armoured brigades (about 330 tanks), took Rostov after a grim struggle with Colonel-General von Kleist. Hitler ordered Rundstedt to stem the retreat of the 1st Panzerarmee in front of the Mius line. Rundstedt promptly requested to be relieved of his command. He was replaced by Reichenau, who made exactly the same arrangements as his predecessor and, what is more, had them accepted by higher authority. All the efforts of the Russian South Front to break the line failed with heavy losses.

Russian army building defences behind retreating Germans.

Soviet sniper with a Tokarev rifle.

The operations order issued for the Transcaucasus Front included two landings in the Crimea: the 51st Army (General Lvov) at Kerch', and the 44th Army (General Chernyak) at Feodosiya. On December 26, only 3,000 Russians were locked in combat with the 46th Division in the Kerch' Peninsula. At dawn on the 29th there were more than 17,000 Russians with 47 guns and 12 tanks, while at the same time advance units of the 44th Army were throwing the Germans into confusion at Feodosiya. Disobeying the express orders of his army commander, General von Sponeck, with his communications in peril, ordered his 46th Division to abandon its positions at Kerch'. When the order was obeyed, all the divisional equipment was left behind. But

Generals Lvov and Chernyak, doubtless inhibited by over-rigid orders, were slow to take up fortune's favours and their hesitation gave Manstein time to bar their road over the Kamenskoye Isthmus. However, to do this he had been obliged to abandon the attack on Sevastopol', with all its consequences. Relieved of his command, Sponeck was court-martialled on Hitler's orders. Without regard for his daring exploits at Rotterdam, where he had led the 22nd Airborne Division, he was sentenced to death. The Führer commuted the sentence to imprisonment in the fortress of Rastatt, where agents of Heinrich Himmler murdered him in the confusion at the end of March 1945.

Guderian gives us the following picture of the winter battle.

He noted it at Tula, but it is true for the whole front:

"On the actual day of the offensive, the thermometer fell from −20 to −40 degrees. The sufferings of the troops were ghastly. All the automatic arms ceased to work because the oil in them froze. On the afternoon of the 5th all the armies called a spontaneous halt.

"There is nothing more dramatic in military history than the stunning assault of the cold on the German Army. The men had greatcoats and jackboots. The only additional clothing they had received consisted of a scarf and a pair of gloves. In the rear, the locomotives had seized up with cold. In the line, weapons were unserviceable and, according to General Schaal, the tank motors had to be warmed up for 12 hours before the machines could get going. One hideous detail is that many men, while satisfying the calls of nature, died when their anuses froze."

On December 20, General Guderian left for the Führer's H.Q. to try and obtain his consent to cease operations. All he got were renewed orders to attack:

"So greatly had the cold disorganised the army that the Führer's orders could not be obeyed. The Russians counterattacked as often as they could, for their own men were suffering badly, but they managed to endanger our forward lines which they trapped by circling round them from behind. Our communications were interrupted and our radio-transmitters put out of action by the snow and the cold. Our casualties were enormous, as the slightest wound meant death. The battle fell silent everywhere, without orders, and in spite of the efforts of the officers."

A solid Soviet defence

Between June 22 and December 6, 1941, Soviet losses in prisoners alone were of the order of 2,800,000 officers, N.C.O.s, and men. From Brest-Litovsk to the suburbs of Moscow, the Germans had covered a distance equivalent to that between London and Prague. But to help it withstand the blows that hammered it, the Red Army possessed two elements lacked by the nations which had been overrun in 1940: depth and resources. Regarding the latter, on December 1, 1941, Stalin is thought to have had at his disposal 200 infantry divisions, 35 cavalry divisions, and 40 armoured brigades (2,600 tanks) at the front, and another 80 formations (63 infantry divisions, six cavalry divisions, and 11 armoured brigades) in the rear. In spite of the difficulties inherent in an operation of that size, the evacuation of war industries to the other side of the Urals was successful and would begin to bear fruit in the spring of 1942. The Soviet Union was now no longer alone. The day after the Germans attacked, President Roosevelt announced that Russia would enjoy the benefits of "Lend-Lease". Winston Churchill shipped no less than 500 Hurricane fighters to his ally on Arctic convoys during the summer and winter of 1941. These supplies would be increased in the following year, in spite of heavy losses suffered by both merchant. men and warships in the convoys.

Eastern Front German troops with howitzer.

On January 1, 1942, between Feodosiya, on the south side of the Crimea, and Oranienbaum on the Gulf of Finland, 12 German armies (with 141 divisions, six of them from satellite countries, plus five Hungarian and Rumanian brigades) were locked in combat with 22 Soviet armies (a total of 328 divisions or their equivalent).

The temperatures of 30 and even 40 degrees below zero, recorded from one end to the other of the front, and 1,000 miles difference in latitude, did not force the Russians to seek winter quarters. On the contrary, during the month of January, Stalin would extend his offensive to the left and right flanks of the front, no longer limiting himself to Army Group "Centre", against which Generals Konev and Zhukov continued to struggle, with 165 divisions confronting Kluge's 68.

In the face of this first Soviet winter offensive, Hitler, who had taken over control of O.K.H. and the Eastern Front from Field-Marshal von Brauchitsch, issued the following order to his armies on December 28.

"The abandonment without struggle of positions, even if they have been only cursorily prepared, leads, under present weather conditions, to intolerable losses in material and munitions. It weakens our fighting capacities and allows the enemy ever-growing freedom of action."

In order to exploit to the full the defensive situation to which he was for the moment reduced, he ordered every village and even every farmhouse to be made into a stronghold, with garrisons drawn from all fighting arms and also from the service échelons. Over a wide expanse of territory, this "quartering" of the terrain — to use General Weygand's expression from the end of May 1940 — would force the enemy to bivouac in the open, prevent him using his road and rail network, and finally reduce him to impotence and famine.

Nevertheless, to redeploy in depth, as the order required, the heavily-stretched German units, who were already fighting on an excessively long front, were obliged to spread their resources even more thinly. And so the enemy was able to filter through the gaps which inevitably opened in their lines. In fact the Russians were able to penetrate the German front even more easily than they would have been able to do in summer, because the extreme temperatures had frozen the lakes and rivers to the extent that they no longer formed obstacles. Their ice was so thick that it could even support 52-ton heavy tanks. To stiffen the German line, which was buckling and threatening to break at any moment, Hitler called on troops from Occupied France and others who had just finished their training in Germany. Between the end of December 1941 and the end of March 1942, no less than 22 infantry divisions were moved from West to East for this purpose.

Moreover, the situation was so dangerous in certain sectors that they were thrown into action just as soon as they arrived, in small groups and without time to distribute equipment and clothing to withstand the climate. For its part, the Red Army was reinforced in the first six months of 1942 by the addition of about 60 new divisions.

The offensive against Army Group "Centre"

In a directive dated January 7, 1942, the Soviet High Command ordered Generals Konev and Zhukov, in command of the Kalinin and West Fronts respectively, to go over once more to the attack, with the intention of annihilating Army Group "Centre".

For this purpose the forces of the Kalinin Front would move forward along the Ostashkov-Volga line, attacking in a general south-westerly direction and, to the west of Vyaz'ma, would cut the road and railway between Minsk and Moscow, the life-lines of Army Group "Centre". Furthermore, using the gap which had been formed during the retreat to the south of Kaluga between the right wing of the German 4th Army and the left wing of 2nd Panzerarmee, the West Front would make its main effort in the direction of Vyaz'ma. This gigantic pincer-movement, aimed at bringing about the encirclement of the whole of Army Group "Centre'; would be covered on its right by attacks by troops of the North-West Front and on its left by offensives by the Bryansk Front.

The offensive so planned made an excellent beginning on January 9 and 10, 1942. For three weeks, O.K.H. was seriously concerned that Konev and Zhukov should meet in the region of Dorogobuzh, some 16 miles south of the Moscow–Minsk railway.

Eremenko pushes through

In the north, the 4th Shock Army (General A. I. Eremenko), which formed the right of the Kalinin Front, took advantage of the thick ice on Lake Seliger, the boundary between Army Groups

"Centre" and "North", to break through the German lines which, in this sector, were no more than skeletal. Eremenko pushed straight as far as Velikiye-Luki, more than 115 miles from his starting-point, replenishing his supplies from depôts which the

Germans had built up at Toropets. In this way the Russians made up for the defects of the Soviet supply services, which had failed to keep up with the front line units. On February 1, however, 3rd Panzerarmee (Colonel-General Reinhardt) retook the line Demidov–Velizh–Nevel'–Velikiye-Luki and blocked the Russians' potentially dangerous advance to Vitebsk and Smolensk.

29th Army cut off

In the centre of the Kalinin Front, General Konev separated his 29th, 39th, and 30th Armies which, to the west of Rzhev, had succeeded in splitting the German 9th Army and isolating its left wing, which consisted of the XXIII Corps (General Schubert). The Soviet 29th Army exploited its breakthrough to the full, and, on January 27, was within tactical reach of the Minsk-Moscow road. But General Walther Model, who had just taken over command of 9th Army, was an astonishing military improviser. Ignoring the various concentrated offensives against Rzhev from the north and east, he counterattacked vigorously in a westerly direction and established contact with XXIII Corps at the end of the month. Now it was the turn of the Soviet 29th Army to find its communications cut. In the course of the subsequent furious battles, it lost 27,000 dead and 5,000 prisoners. Only 5,000 men, 800 of whom were wounded, managed to break out of the pocket and reach Soviet lines on February 15.

"German casualties, too, had been heavy," Paul Carell notes. "On February 18, when Obersturmbannführer Otto Kumm reported at his divisional headquarters, Model happened to be there. He said to Kumm: 'I know what your regiment has been through — but I still can't do without it. What is its present strength?'

"Kumm gestured towards the window. 'Herr Generaloberst, my regiment is on parade outside.' Model glanced through the window. Outside, 35 men had fallen in."

Model's gift for manoeuvre and his prompt decision had therefore carried the day against Russian doggedness, for the Russian 39th Army was as sore-hit as the Germans. Nevertheless, Model's army was trapped in a tube-shaped pocket nearly 125 miles long and, in the region of Sychevka, barely 40 miles in width.

It was now vital that Rzhev be evacuated, if only to allow the 12 or so divisions earmarked for the summer offensive the chance to recuperate. Yet before he would consent, Hitler delayed until the reverse at Stalingrad set the seal on his defeat.

Hitler consents to a retreat

On the other hand, on January 15, in view of the speedy and dangerous advances by the 49th, 50th, and 10th Armies of the West Front into the breach which had been opened south of Kaluga, Hitler authorised Kluge to order the necessary withdrawals to permit the left of 2nd Panzerarmee to link-up firmly again with the right of 4th Army:

"This is the first time in the war," his order concluded, "that

I have ordered a withdrawal over a sizeable section of the front. I expect the movement to be carried out in a manner worthy of the German Army. Our men's confidence in their innate superiority and their absolute determination to cause the enemy as much damage as possible must also condition the way in which this withdrawal is carried out."

In order to slow down enemy pursuit, the Germans, just as the Russians had done previously, applied a scorched earth policy to the areas they abandoned. Villages were razed, and even the stoves used to heat the Russian dwellings were destroyed at Hitler's express order.

Zhukov's advance blocked

General Zhukov's offensive followed a pattern similar to Konev's. A lightning jump-off took I Guard Cavalry Corps almost to Dorogobuzh, but there the advance was checked, causing a stabilised front to develop. At the end of February, Field-Marshal von Kluge had redeployed after his withdrawal and re-established a continuous front along the Kirov-Yukhnov line. As a result, General Pliev's I Guard Cavalry Corps was trapped and, slightly more to the north, a similar fate overtook the 33rd Army. Russian G.H.Q. in Moscow tried to get the operation moving again by parachuting two brigades behind the German lines and extending General Zhukov's authority to include the Kalinin Front.

Eastern Front Russian T34 tank.

But Army Group "Centre" still maintained its positions along the Minsk–Vyaz'ma and Vyaz'ma–Rzhev lines.

The History of the Great Patriotic War does not conceal the slowing down of this winter offensive, from which Stalin had expected a decisive victory. It blames its failure on to the fact that the armies of the West Front wasted their shock value by attacking over fronts which were too long. This is very likely, but the question must be considered at a higher level than the one set by the Great Patriotic War. It would appear that the principles of concentration of force and convergence of effort were both insufficiently understood in the highest councils of Stavka, as Russian G.H.Q. was called.

Beginning on January 8, to the north of the Kalinin Front, General Kurochkin, commander of the North-West Front, badly mauled the German 16th Army, which formed the right wing of Army Group "Centre". The 16th Army broke under the assault of the 3rd Shock Army (General Purkaev) emerging from the Lake Seliger region, and the 11th Army (General Morosov), which swept over the frozen Lake Ilmen.

Certainly the latter, in spite of five furious attacks, was halted before Staraya Russa, but working its way up the Lovat' it succeeded, on February 8, in closing the trap around the German II Corps. This formed a 200 mile pocket around Dem'yansk, which was defended by five badly worn divisions. But, under the command of General Brockdorff-Ahlefeldt, they repelled every enemy attack, even when the Russians parachuted two brigades into the centre of the pocket. To supply the 96,000 men and their 20,000 horses, the Luftwaffe organised an airlift. At a rate of 100 to 150 aircraft daily, it brought the besieged men more than 65,000 tons of foodstuffs, forage, munitions, and fuel, also flying out over 34,500 wounded and sick.

Failure before Leningrad

Under the command of General Vlasov, 2nd Shock Army, six divisions strong, crossed the Volkhov on January 22 and pushed north-east, reaching the Leningrad–Novgorod railway. The attack was to take place at the same time as an offensive by the 54th Army, emerging from the area south-east of Petrokrepost'. If the manoeuvre had succeeded, the salient formed here by the German 18th Army would have been liquidated and Leningrad relieved at the same time. But the 54th Army failed in the face of the resistance of I Corps (March 10, 1942).

From that moment on, Vlasov, who had been reinforced by the XIII Cavalry Corps and three armoured brigades and had deployed his forces fanwise, found himself in a very risky situation, for the handle of the fan was only 13 miles wide while his forward troops were 50 miles from the Volkhov. From March 15 to March 19, furious combat, in which the Spanish volunteers of the División Azul distinguished themselves, allowed the German 18th Army to sever the line which joined the 2nd Shock Army to the main Soviet line. The mopping-up operations lasted until the end of May. Vlasov himself was not captured until the end of July.,

Success in the south

In the southern theatre of operations, the sudden death of Field-Marshal von Reichenau led Hitler to entrust the command of Army Group "South" to Field-Marshal von Bock. As he entered his office at Poltava on January 18, the new commander of German operations in the Ukraine and the Crimea was received with two pieces of news. One was good: Feodosiya had been recaptured by General von Manstein, who had also taken 10,000 prisoners. This would allow the siege of Sevastopol' to continue without fear of being surprised by Russian attack. The other news was disturbing: the 17th Army's front had been pierced near Izyum.

General von Manstein recalls the difficulties which arose at the time of the recapture of Feodosiya and also his attitude about the treatment of Russian P.O.W.s:

"Everything seemed to have conspired against us. Extremely severe frosts affected the airfields at Simferopol' and Yevpatoriya, which were used by our Stukas and bombers, and often prevented aircraft taking off in the morning to attack Feodosiya. The Kerch' Strait was frozen over and allowed free passage to enemy units.

"In spite of the difficulties, the army did its best to feed- sometimes even reducing its own rations-the prisoners whom we had not sufficient transport to transfer north. Consequently, the mortality rate among the prisoners averaged only two per cent. This was an extremely low figure, considering that most of them were seriously wounded or absolutely exhausted at the time of their capture. One incident may serve to illustrate their feelings towards us. There was a camp for 8,000 prisoners close to Feodosiya when the Russians made their landing. The camp guards fled, but the prisoners, instead of running towards their 'liberators', set off, without guards, towards Simferopol', towards us, that is."

On the Donets, Marshal Timoshenko, in command of the South-West Front, had attacked seven German divisions with his 37th, 57th, and 6th Armies, totalling 21 infantry divisions, 11 cavalry divisions, and ten armoured brigades (about 650 tanks). The long-range object of this operation was Khar'kov and the railway between Dniepropetrovsk and Donetsk (Stalino), which supplied the German 17th Army and 1st Panzerarmee. In temperatures of 40 degrees below zero the Russians spread out behind the German line and, by January 26, were restocking their supplies from the stores which the 17th Army had established at Lozovaya. Two days later they reached Sinel'nikovo and Grishino, which were within gunshot of the railway they hoped to cut. Several days later they were thrown back by Gruppe von Kleist which was an amalgamation of Kleist's own 1st Panzerarmee and the 17th Army.

The Russian attack then folded up. Army Group "South" had indeed had a nasty shock, but Timoshenko had not been able to widen the breach he had made on the Donets front on January 18. The Izyum salient, about 60 miles deep, would cause him the same tragic disaster as the Volkhov salient had brought on Vlasov.

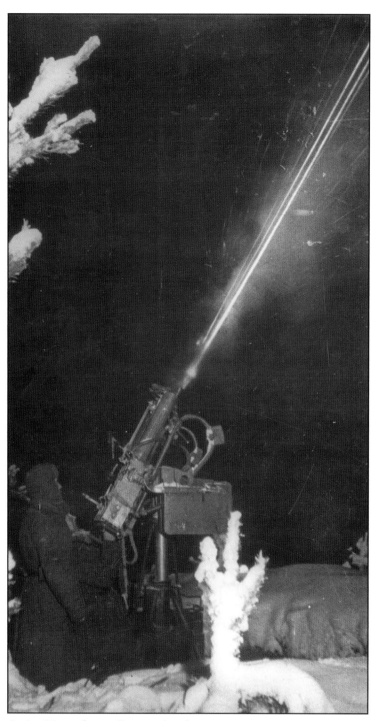

Soviet AA gun fires at German aircraft.

In his H.Q. at Poltava, Bock had chosen May 18 for Operation "Fridericus I", a pincer movement intended to take the Izyum salient as ordered. But at dawn on May 12 he learned that his 6th Army (General Paulus) was itself being heavily attacked around Khar'kov. A few hours later it became clear that it was not simply a local attack but a major strategic offensive employing dozens of divisions and hundreds of tanks.

At the end of the winter, Stalin and his advisers in Moscow had refused to accept that they should remain on the defensive when spring came. On the contrary, they intended to attack. The Great Patriotic War includes this justifiable comment on their decision: "The Supreme Command G.H.Q. exaggerated the success of the counter-attack and ordered a general offensive in all important sectors, thus scattering their reserves."

Anyhow, at the end of March, Stavka rejected, because of lack of reserves, a plan put forward by Marshal Timoshenko which would have brought Russian forces back to the Dniepr between Gomel' and Cherkassy, and between Cherkassy and Nikolayev on the right bank of the river. Instead, they placed the South and South-West Fronts under his command, and gave him the much more modest objective of Khar'kov.

Khruschev is sent to Stalin

Timoshenko divided his forces into two. North, in the Volchansk area, the 28th Army (Lieutenant-General D. I. Ryabyshev) reinforced to 16 infantry and three cavalry divisions, and six armoured brigades, was to break through the German front and exploit its success towards the south-west. In the south, the 6th Army (Lieutenant-General A. M. Gorodnyansky: 11 infantry and six cavalry divisions, and 13 tank brigades) would break out of the Izyum salient, attack south of Khar'kov, and having broken through, then converge on the north-west, moving in front of Ryabyshev. Finally, cavalry and armoured forces would advance quickly on Dniepropetrovsk.

In the Volchansk sector, the 28th Army's attack, launched on May 9, was checked after having pushed out a salient of some 20 miles into the enemy lines. In the south, on the other hand, Gorodnyansky set General Paulus and Field-Marshal von Bock a very worrying problem. On May 14 VIII Corps was nearly in ruins; on May 16 the Russians arrived at Merefa and Karlovka on the heels of the 454th Security Division, which had given ground, and a Hungarian division which had done no better. Sixty-four guns had also been lost.

In these circumstances, could Operation "Fridericus" retrieve the situation? Paulus and Bock doubted it very much, and on May 14 the latter noted in his diary: "Although I am most unwilling to do this, I can only propose, as far as the Army Group is concerned, to grab from Kleist [right prong of the "Fridericus" pincer] everything we can get hold of, say three or four divisions, one of them armoured, and transport them to XI Panzer Corps' left flank. From there they will attack the southern flank of the enemy pocket."

In agreement for once, Hitler and Halder were intractable. Colonel-General von Kleist managed to save a day on his timetable and counter-attack at dawn on May 17. He fell on the Russian 9th and 57th Armies (South Front) under Major-General F. M. Kharitonov and Lieutenant-General K. P. Podlas, who had to protect the offensive by the South-West Front from surprise attacks. It is true that Kharitonov had only four divisions to hold a 65-mile front and that Luftflotte IV was applying its usual great pressure.

It took no miracle therefore for Gruppe von Kleist, with 15 divisions, including four Rumanian, to reach the Donets within 48 hours. Faced with this unexpected reversal, Timoshenko asked the Supreme Command to authorise the abandonment of the Khar'kov attack. This was refused, so he appealed to Stalin through N. S. Khruschev, political member of the council of South-West Front. During the 20th Congress of the Communist Party of the Soviet Union in February 1956, Khruschev explained this fruitless attempt. "Against all good sense Stalin rejected our proposal and ordered that the Khar'kov operation must continue; and yet several of our army units were already threatened with encirclement and extermination … I telephoned the Chief-of-Staff, Vasilevsky, and begged him to explain the situation to Comrade Stalin. But Vasilevsky replied that Comrade Stalin wanted to hear no more about it. So I telephoned Stalin at his villa. It was Malenkov who replied. I said I wanted to speak to Stalin personally. Stalin's answer was that I could speak to Malenkov. Again I asked for Stalin himself. But he continued to refuse, though he was only a few steps from the telephone. After having 'listened', so to speak, to our request Stalin ordered: 'Leave things as they are.' And what was the result? The worst one could expect-our armies were surrounded by the Germans and we lost hundreds of thousands of men."

German attack Sevastopol'.

The fall of Sevastopol'

The striking victory at Kerch' had freed the German 11th Army from any pressure on its rear, so Manstein was able to start the attack on Sevastopol' on June 7. He had received very strong reinforcements: three assault gun units, 24 Nebelwerfer rocket-launching batteries, and most of the siege artillery in general reserve. Amongst the last were two 60-cm Karl mortars and the 80-cm super-heavy Gustav railway gun, which fired seven-ton shells at the rate of three an hour. This monster's barrel was 100 feet long and weighed 130 tons. In addition, the Luftwaffe had provided 600 aircraft, including General von Richthofen's Stukas.

It was, nevertheless, a hard nut to crack. Commanded by General I. E. Petrov, the Sevastopol' garrison had seven divisions, plus one unmounted cavalry division and Vice-Admiral F. S. Oktyabrsky's three brigades of marines. It depended on 3,600 permanent or temporary fortified positions set up in depth over some 15 miles. Amongst these was the Maxim Gorky fort, with four 305-mm guns in two turrets. The Russians had no opposition for the enemy's overwhelming air power, however.

Manstein's attack involved three corps, including the Rumanian mountain corps, in all nine divisions, including two Rumanian. LIV Corps had the main task, to attack on the northern front, while XXX Corps with stronger forces took the southern front. It has been calculated that the German artillery fired about 46,700 tons of shells, and that the Luftwaffe dropped

125,000 bombs during 25,000 sorties in one month. But for all that, the defenders were not intimidated. Each attack had to be decided by close hand-to-hand combat. When German infantry and pioneers had overrun the portions of any particular fort above the ground, they had then to overcome resistance in the labyrinth of underground installations, with the risk of being blown up with the defenders. And with destroyers and submarines the Black Sea Fleet worked hard to reinforce and supply the garrison. But although the German 11th Army's progress was slow, it was still sure and relentless.

On June 27, LIV Corps reached the north side of North Bay, and during the night of June 28 and 29 got its 22nd Airborne Division across in motor assault craft. XXX Corps had taken the dominating heights of Sapun. Sevastopol' was lost, but the defenders still gave the 11th Army a hard task. On July 4 Hitler had made Colonel-General von Manstein a Field-Marshal, but he had to wait until July 9 before the last stubborn resistance in the Khersonesskiy peninsula was overcome, fighting to the last cartridge and the last drop of water.

The Germans lost 24,111 killed and wounded, but captured 95,000 prisoners and 467 guns. The Germans were now in possession of the whole Crimea except the southern mountains, where there were still partisans, and the 11th Army was now available for other tasks.

Meanwhile the German 6th Army, not satisfied with having overcome the Izyum and Volchansk bridgeheads, itself crossed the Donets to secure a good jumping off position on the Oskol, the left bank tributary of this important waterway. This part of

"Fridericus" brought in 45,000 prisoners, 266 tanks, and 208 guns.

According to Halder's table, already referred to, Field-Marshal von Bock had on June 16, between the Kerch' Strait and the Kursk area, 73 divisions of all types, including nine Panzer, seven motorised (two of them Waffen S.S.), and 26 satellite divisions. If the Great Patriotic War is to be believed, Stalin drew no conclusions from this impressive concentration of forces. Thus we read: "The Soviet High Command of course thought it possible that the Wehrmacht might attack in the south. It considered however that the enemy would not make its main attack on Stalingrad and the Caucasus but, with its forces before Moscow, would try to outflank the centre groups of the Red Army and take Moscow and the central industrial area."

Hence, in this author's view, Stavka's mistaken decisions during the first part of the summer campaign. Priority was given to reinforcements for the Bryansk Front which, if broken, would have let the enemy through to Tula and the capital. There is no doubt that this is what happened. But according to Accoce's La guerre a été gagnée en Suisse, the Soviet agent Rudolf Rössler had, from Lucerne, transmitted the text of Directive No. 41 to his superiors in Moscow. This was on April 14, ten days after Hitler had signed it. On May 3 Colonel-General Halder wrote this note: "Exchange Telegraph in Moscow is sending out surprising reports about our intentions."

Also, on June 20, eight days before the attack, a Fieseler Storch crashed behind the Russian lines while on its way back to the 23rd Panzer Division H.Q. In the aircraft, Major Reichel had apparently been carrying completely detailed operations orders for XL Corps. One can conclude that Stalin had therefore received more than enough information about enemy intentions from his Intelligence, but that he had ignored their reports. Why? Perhaps he thought he was being deliberately misled by the enemy, and clung more than ever to the belief that Moscow was to be the main objective of the coming German offensive.

Breakthrough on the Don

On June 28 Gruppe von Weichs attacked on a 90-mile front with its left south of Orel and its right at Oboyan. Colonel-General von Weichs sent in his own 2nd Army, the 4th Panzerarmee (Colonel-General Hoth), and the Hungarian 2nd Army (Colonel-General Jany), in all 23 divisions, including three Panzer and two motorised.

Two days later it was the turn of Paulus's 6th Army, which extended the attack another 50 miles, with 18 divisions, including two Panzer and one motorised. Paulus's XL Corps (3rd and 23rd Panzer Divisions and 29th Motorised Division) was to close the pincer with Hoth. It was a striking success. The left of the Bryansk Front (General Golikov) and the right of the South-West Front were broken. On July 1 the Panzers were at Stary-Oskol and reached Valuyki on July 3, while one of General Hoth's divisions stormed a bridge over the Don and pushed into Voronezh. This created a pocket in which 30,000 Russians were taken prisoner.

The Don-Donets corridor was therefore opened up according to the plan adopted on April 5. The Germans were to exploit this opening with Hoth and Paulus rolling through it to meet the 1st

Panzerarmee (Colonel-General von Kleist), preparing to attack north-east across the Donets. Though fearing a counter-attack on his flank, Bock nevertheless kept his 4th Panzerarmee around Voronezh. This act of timidity cost him his command; on July 15 Colonel-General von Weichs took over Army Group "B", leaving his own 2nd Army, already in defensive positions on the Orel-Voronezh front, to General H. von Salmuth.

In spite of this error the 6th Army still moved on towards the great curve of the Don and threatened to overrun the South-West Front. This brought an order from Timoshenko on July 7 for a retreat. It meant that Army Group "A", attacking two days later, met only rearguards when crossing the Don. Field-Marshal List's forces, from left to right, were the 1st Panzerarmee (Kleist) and Gruppe Ruoff (17th Army and the Italian 8th Army) that is another 24 German, five Rumanian, three Italian, and one Slovak (including four Panzer and four motorised) divisions.

At the same time, Paulus was arriving at Rossosh' and a gigantic pincer movement was taking shape between Voronezh and Rostov, involving 52 divisions, including 18 armoured and motorised (about 2,300 tanks). On July 12 List extended his operation to the Sea of Azov, broke through the enemy lines at Krasnyy Luch, and five days later took Voroshilovgrad. This new setback, to say the least, forced Stalin to order Lieutenant-General R. Ya. Malinovsky, commander of South Front, to fall back in his turn. He perhaps intended to bar the enemy's way to the bend of the Don along a line from Voronezh to Rostov, but in this case he had not appreciated the weakened state of his own forces and the offensive momentum of the Panzers.

Germans among ruins of Sebastopol.

So on July 15 Hoth and his Panzerarmee took Millerovo, having covered half the distance to Stalingrad in three weeks. In view of this situation, the next day Halder called together the heads of his Intelligence and Operations sections to discuss the possibility of lunging for Stalingrad without waiting for the fall of Rostov. He was thus remaining faithful to the spirit of the April 5 directive, while Hitler was moving further away from it.

Fearing that the 1st Army might run into difficulties at Rostov, the Führer, from July 13, had placed Hoth, now reinforced by XL Corps, under Army Group "A"; then he had ordered it to swing from east to south-east. This brought it on July 17 to Tsimlyansk, upstream from the junction of the Donets and the Don, while

Kleist himself had forced the Donets at Kamensk-Shakhtinskiy. Hitler remained deaf to the warnings from Halder and thought he was going to be able to pull off a massive encircling movement as successful as those at Kiev and Bryansk-Vyaz'ma in 1941, thus opening up the way to the Caucasus and pulling off the great strategic coup of which he dreamed.

An enormous bottleneck and major supply difficulties then built up. But above all, without XL Corps' armoured and motorised strength, the 6th Army remained the only force still making for Stalingrad, instead of the two army groups as originally planned. Hoth's transfer prevented him from exploiting his newly-won bridgeheads on the southern Don and striking to the Volga. Paulus, having to depend on his own resources, was forced to mark time while the enemy were using every means in their power to organise quickly a new Stalingrad Front.

Moreover, Paulus himself was far from overjoyed with the situation. Talking after the battle with his son Ernest Alexander, who had been wounded in a tank, he told him: "You can see the damage your tanks inflicted on the Russians. There are heaps of their tanks destroyed on the battlefield. We were told this story by a captured Russian officer — Timoshenko had been watching a tank battle from an observation post, and when he saw the rate at which his tanks were literally shot to pieces by their opponents he went pale and left, muttering 'It's frightful, frightful'." However, the wounded son sensed concern rather than satisfaction behind his father's spirited account of events. Paulus was certainly wondering what new reserves might be produced by the enemy who seemed, like Lerna's hydra, to sprout new heads as soon as the old ones were cut off.

On July 23 Rostov fell to Colonel-General von Kleist, but did not yield the expected amount of prisoners and booty. Hitherto in a state of depression, Hitler, again for no good reason, became once more optimistic. Hence his Directive No. 45, to carry out Operation "Braunschweig". It was signed on July 23 at his new H.Q., set up at Vinnitsa in the western Ukraine to enable him to keep a closer watch on the current offensive. In his preamble he proclaimed: "In a three-week campaign the main objectives

T-34 + T-26 Russian tanks support Soviet ski troops.

I had indicated behind the southern wing of the Eastern Front have been achieved. Only remnants of Timoshenko's armies have managed to escape encirclement and reach the south bank of the Don. It must be admitted that they will be reinforced from the Caucasus. The concentration of another group of armies is taking place near Stalingrad, where the enemy is likely to make a stubborn defence."

The July 23 directive has since the war found no defenders on the German side. All the West German military historians' accounts consulted agree that the disaster which followed was the direct result of the decision imposed on the High Command by Hitler. To quote just one writer, the former chief-of-staff of LII Corps, Major-General Hans Doerr, who took part in the campaign with Army Group "A": "This July 23 must be considered as the day it became clear that the German Supreme Command abandoned standard principles of warfare to adopt peculiar new approaches stemming rather from Adolf Hitler's irrational and diabolical power than from methodical and realistic military practice. Once again history proved that Faith and the Devil triumphed over Reason. The trained soldiers around Hitler were virtually impotent, under the spell of the Devil."

Of course Russian historians do not agree with Major-General Doerr's view. One can only quote here the opinion of Marshal A. I. Eremenko, former commander of the Stalingrad Front. He writes: "German generals will not succeed in proving that if Hitler had not forced them to get bogged down in the battle for Stalingrad they would have achieved victory and in any case would have taken the Caucasus in the autumn of 1942. The most important issue was not that Hitler was thrusting simultaneously towards both Stalingrad and the Caucasus, but that he had insufficient forces to fight both battles successfully. He had imposed this impossible task on his army to prove to satellites and potential allies the strength of the Wehrmacht (it was thus assumed that victory at Stalingrad and in the Caucasus would force Turkey, in the south, and Japan, in the Far East, to declare war on the U.S.S.R.)."

The Germans approach Stalingrad

Whatever the weakness of the Soviet forces barring his way to Stalingrad, Field-Marshal von Weichs, as a result of the July 23 directive, had only the 6th Army to break through them. But even this was not complete since Paulus was waiting for the Italian 8th Army (General Gariboldi) to extend the line from the Hungarian 2nd Army (General Jany) on the Don, and meanwhile had to cover his flank with his own forces. Again, fuel was in short supply and he could not use all his armour at once. This explains his slow progress from the bridgehead he had taken on July 20 at Bokovskaya on the Chir. On July 30 Hitler returned the 4th Panzerarmee to Army Group "B", but Hoth, on receiving his new orders, was over 90 miles to the south-west of Tsimlyansk, and his orders were to move towards Stalingrad by the left bank of the Don.

On August 4 the 6th Army was nevertheless at Kalach at the top of the river bend, but the Russian 1st Tank Army (Major-General K. S. Moskalenko) got across the river and put up a stubborn resistance which lasted a week.

Paulus finally overcame it with a pincer movement. His XIV Panzer Corps (General G. von Wietersheim) pushed from north to south to meet the XXIV Panzer Corps (General W. von Langermann and Erlenkamp) in the enemy's rear. A brilliant success, but the 6th Army was not able to exploit it until August 21.

On that day LI Corps, magnificently supported by Luftflotte IV and with insignificant casualties, established two bridgeheads on the eastern bank of the Don, upstream of Kalach. On the evening of August 23 the 16th Panzer Division, leading the XIV Panzer Corps, arrived at Rynok on the west bank of the Volga after a thrust of over 30 miles. Wietersheim was counter-attacked furiously from north and south and wanted to retreat. Consequently he received the order to hand over his corps to Lieutenant-General Hube, commander of the 16th Panzer Division. A well-timed action by VIII Corps (General W. Heitz) relieved XIV Panzer Corps and made a defensive front possible between the Don and the Volga upstream from Stalingrad. LI Corps followed up its success towards the south-east, which allowed Paulus to combine his operations with Hoth's.

Making for the bend in the Volga by way of the left bank of the Don, Hoth had been reduced to six divisions, of which one was armoured and one motorised. It is not surprising therefore that with such slender resources he was stopped at the exit from Abganerovo on August 10. As Army Group "B" had no reserves it was up to Paulus to help them out, and he transferred his 297th Division and 24th Panzer Division. This was made possible by his success at Kalach. This reinforcement meant that the 4th Panzerarmee could renew the attack on Tinguta, but it was not enough for them to reach the heights overlooking the Volga downstream from Stalingrad. Failing further reinforcements, Hoth switched XLVIII Panzer Corps from his right to his left and pushed it due north. On September 2 he made contact with the 6th Army's right at Voroponvo.

In his attack orders on August 19, Colonel-General Paulus assigned the objective of the south and centre of Stalingrad to LI Corps, and the northern districts to XIV Panzer Corps. The latter could spare only a fraction of its forces for this task because, with VIII Corps, it had to cover the 6th Army in the Volga-Don isthmus. It was not appreciated that this town, which then had 445,000 inhabitants, extended over 20 miles along the Volga and that, in places, there were five miles between the river banks and the western edge of the town.

The assault on Stalingrad This makeshift attack could only suc ceed if it met an enemy which was not only beaten but whose morale was extremely low. From the very first engagements in the streets of Stalingrad it was clear to the Germans that the Russians had recovered beyond anyone's expectations, and that the Russians' slogan "The Volga has only one bank" was no empty boast. On September 16 Colonel-General von Richthofen, now commander of Luftflotte IV, complaining of the lack of spirit in the 6th Army, wrote in his diary: "With a little enthusiastic effort, the town should fall in two days." Less than a week later, he noted, more justly: "September 22. In the town itself progress is desperately slow. The 6th Army will never finish the job at this rate. Above all because it is threatened from the north by the Russians and because reinforcements arrive only in dribs and drabs. We have to fight endless engagements, taking one cellar after another in order to gain any ground at all."

At the same time, in the Caucasus, Army Group "A" 's offensive reached what Clausewitz called a falling-off point, beyond which wear and tear take over from the initial drive and energy.

The day after the fall of Rostov, Field-Marshal List's only worries were about supplies. It was impossible to satisfy the needs of 26 advancing divisions, some moving south-west, some south, and some south-east-so much so that Colonel-General von Kleist jested: "No Russians in front of us; no supplies behind us!" Jerricans of petrol dropped from Junkers Ju 52 transports had to be brought to the Panzers by camel transport.

In spite of these logistic difficulties Gruppe Ruoff (German 17th Army and Rumanian 3rd Army) occupied simultaneously on August 9 the port of Yeysk on the south bank of the Sea of Azov, Krasnodar on the Kuban', and Maykop (whose oil

wells had been so thoroughly sabotaged that they were not in operation again until four years after the war). On the same day the 1st Panzerarmee took Pyatigorsk at the bottom of the first foothills of the Caucasus; on its left, the 16th Motorised Division positioned itself at Elista in the centre of the Kalmuk Steppe and sent out patrols towards Astrakhan'. On August 21 a combined detachment (to avoid jealousies) of the 1st and 4th Gebirgsjäger Divisions scaled Mount El' brus (over 17,000 feet), while at the end of the month Kleist crossed the Terek not far from Prokhladnyy, some 80 miles from the Grozny oil wells.

It is true that the nearer they got to their respective objectives (Batumi and Baku), the more List's two groups became separated, and thus found themselves unable to co-ordinate their operations. In addition, Ruoff's outflanking movements over the mountains, intended to overcome resistance on the coast, became increasingly difficult as he moved south-east. On September 6 he succeeded in taking Novorossiysk, but he then had to reorganise his forces before tackling Tuapse.

Russian Cossacks charge enemy.

According to Soviet historians, their country's Anglo-Saxon allies were feckless in the pursuit of victory. The second front was slow in coming and they did no better when it came to furnishing the arms, equipment, petrol and raw materials which shortly after Hitler's invasion the Soviet Union had been assured of receiving.

But it is only proper to note that this accusation can only be made to stand up by comparing the number of tanks, planes etc. that Churchill and Roosevelt had promised to Stalin with those that actually arrived in Russia, while, injustice the comparison ought to be made between the quantities promised and those which were embarked in American and British ports. For what was lost en route can scarcely be attributed to bad faith on the part of London or Washington. To get such supplies to the Soviet Union, Britain and America had the choice of three routes:

1. They could go via Vladivostok, through which Britain, could send sizeable quantities of tin and rubber from Malaya to Siberia. After the opening of hostilities in the Far East, as we have noted, the Japanese did not stop Russian vessels plying between Vladivostok and America's Pacific ports. However, the Trans-Siberian Railway was capable at this time of carrying little more than it had been able to do at the beginning of the century.

2. There was the Persian Gulf route, which had become available on the occupation of Persia by Anglo-Soviet forces at the end of August 1941. But supplies flowed along these two lines very feebly and thought was now given to making significant improvements in them by sending out a large contingent of American engineers and technicians. Nevertheless, the Allied merchantmen taking this route and sailing from New York or Liverpool still had to round the Cape of Good Hope, which put the American Atlantic ports at 73 days sailing from Bandar-e-Shahpur on the Persian Gulf.

3. Lastly, there was the Arctic route to Archangel and Murmansk. The first of these two ports is inaccessible in winter and, anyway, was badly equipped in 1942. The other, thanks to the Gulf Stream, is open all the year round and, given the circumstances, was somewhat better fitted out.

During the winter, Allied Arctic convoys benefited form the cover of the long Arctic night. On the other hand, the advance of pack ice towards the south forced them to round North Cape at a distance which laid them open to short-range German attacks. In summer, the, retreat of the ice allowed the convoys to stand further off from the Norwegian coast, but for 24 hours out of 24 they were, if discovered, an easy prey to dive-bomber, torpedo aircraft, and submarine attacks.

On the outward journey these convoys were distinguished by the letter P.Q. followed by their sequence number. The ships, which were unloaded at Murmansk and Archangel, waited there until they were numerous enough to be regrouped as a Q.P. convoy, and raised anchor when the escort ships of an incoming convoy could accompany them on the voyage home.

The first Arctic convoys

Convoys P.Q.1 set sail from Scottish waters on September 29, 1941, and before the end of the year five others had followed it, landing in all 120,000 tons of supplies at Murmansk, including

600 tanks, 800 aircraft, and 1,400 motor vehicles. Opponents of Winston Churchill's war strategy claim that these supplies would have sufficed to check the Japanese at Singapore and to defeat Rommel at Tobruk. Whatever the truth of this assertion, it has to be admitted that the Germans found themselves considerably embarrassed by these first convoys, which they had not foreseen. It is also noteworthy that between September 29 and December 31, 1941, all 55 vessels of the first six convoys reached their destination safely.

During the first half of 1942 no less than ten convoys made the Arctic run, and of their 146 cargo vessels, 128 reached port despite the increasing opposition of the German Navy. As we have already seen, Hitler had feared an Anglo-American landing in Norway and in consequence had stationed the 43,000-ton battleship Tirpitz, the pocket battleships Lutzow and Admiral Scheer, the heavy cruiser Admiral Hipper, and a dozen U-boats between Trondheim and Narvik. And, at the return of spring, Luftflotte V had at its bases around the North Cape more than 250 machines, including 130 Junkers Ju 87 and 88 bombers and 60 land and seaplane torpedo aircraft.

Faced by this concentration of forces, the Admiralty was forced to provide the same protection for the Arctic convoys as for the Mediterranean ones. Yet at the same time it was the Admiralty which had to bear the brunt of the battle of the Atlantic — and after having just improvised another fleet for the Far East.

In consequence, the situation was very precarious, especially

First of the Atlantic Convoys to Murmansk.

since Roosevelt continued to urge Churchill to intensify and speed up the provisioning of the Soviet Union. And to this end he attached Task Force 99 (Rear-Admiral R. C. Giffen) to the Home Fleet, with two 35,000-ton battleships, the aircraft-carrier Wasp, two heavy cruisers, and a flotilla of destroyers.

At the beginning of March Tirpitz came out to intercept and destroy the convoys P.Q. 12 and Q.P. 8, a total of 31 cargo vessels, but because of inadequate aerial reconnaissance the powerful battleship failed to locate her prey. The hunter now became the hunted, since the Home Fleet, which had been detailed to provide strategic cover for the operation, had not failed to notice Tirpitz's movements; and on the morning of March 9 she was attacked by 12 torpedo-planes from Victorious. However, the undeniable bravery of the Fleet Air Arm pilots did not make up for their lack of training. None of the torpedoes hit its target.

Success for the Luftwaffe The next convoy to arrive at Murmansk, between March 30 and April 1, lost five ships on the way. The U-boats and the Luftwaffe claimed two each, and the fifth went to a division of destroyers which had put out from the port of Kirkenes. But the Germans paid for this success with the loss of the destroyer Z-26 and the U-boats U-585 and U-655. In the course of the encounter that led to the sinking of Z-26 the British cruiser Trinidad was damaged by one of her own torpedoes and had to put into Murmansk.

At the end of April the protection of P.Q. 15, with its 15 merchant vessels, occasioned the loss of the cruiser Edinburgh, torpedoed by U-450 and finished off two days later by destroyer attack. For its part, Trinidad left Murmansk again only to be sunk by a Junkers Ju 88, and to crown misfortunes, in the fog, the battleship King George V rammed the destroyer Punjabi, which sank within a few minutes, though not before her exploding depth-charges had damaged King George V severely.

As the days lengthened the losses of the convoys mounted, despite the reinforcement of their escorts with anti-aircraft vessels bristling with A.A. guns, and C.A.M. ships, merchantmen from which a Hurricane fighter could be catapulted into the air. Of the 35 vessels that made up P.Q. 16, which set sail from the base at Hvalfjord, north of Reykjavik, seven fell into the ambushes prepared for them by the Luftwaffe and U-boats.

However disappointing they may have been, these losses were slight when compared with the catastrophe which overtook P.Q. 17, a disaster not only on account of the strength of the attack to which it succumbed, but also because of the unfortunate intervention of the First Lord of the Admiralty, Admiral of the Fleet Sir Dudley Pound.

Convoy P.Q. 17 was composed of 35 vessels, 22 of which were American, eight British, two Russian, two Panamanian, and one Dutch. It set sail from the Bay of Reykjavik on June 27, 1942, with an escort of six destroyers, four corvettes, four armed trawlers, three mine-sweepers, two submarines and two auxiliary anti-aircraft vessels. Further support was given by Rear-Admiral L. H. K. Hamilton's squadron, which comprised four heavy cruisers, two of which were American, and three destroyers. Finally, Admiral Sir John Tovey had ordered the Home Fleet to sea, bringing together under his command the battleships Duke of York and Washington (U.S.N.), the aircraft-carrier Victorious, the cruisers Nigeria and Cumberland, and 14 destroyers. The Admiralty had done things in style.

Discovered on July 1, the convoy lost three merchant vessels on July 4, all to torpedoes dropped by German Heinkel 111's. By the evening of that same day the convoy was still about 280 miles away from Archangel by way of the North Cape — for Murmansk had been almost completely destroyed by repeated bomber attacks by Luftflotte V.

The Admiralty was now informed that Tirpitz had joined Scheer and Hipper in Altenfjord, which led to the inference that a powerful enemy formation would attack the convoy and Rear-Admiral Hamilton's supporting escort around dawn next day and would swiftly destroy them. Upon which, after brief deliberation, Sir Dudley Pound sent out these three messages, which sealed the convoy's fate.

"2111 Hours: Most immediate. Cruiser force withdraw to westward at high speed.

"2123 Hours: Immediate. Owing to the threat of surface ships convoy is to disperse and proceed to Russian ports.

"2136 Hours: Most Immediate. My 2123 of the 4th. Convoy is to scatter."

On receiving these orders Rear-Admiral Hamilton retired at the indicated speed, taking with him the six escort destroyers. The convoy dispersed as ordered. But of the 30 merchantmen which were left to make Archangel by themselves only 11 arrived at their destination between July 11 and July 25, some of them having made off eastwards towards Novaya Zemlya to escape their pursuers. Nine cargo ships fell prey to air attack from Luftflotte

V and ten to the 82 torpedoes fired by the U-boats involved. The Germans lost only two bombers, three torpedo planes, and two reconnaissance aircraft.

Tirpitz and her companions, escorted by six destroyers, left Altenfjord at 1100 hours on July 5, more than 12 hours after Hitler had given his permission. But they did not get far, for the same day, at 2200 hours, they were ordered to return to base immediately.

As may be expected, this tragic episode gave rise to passionate dispute in Great Britain, and, as Captain Roskill judiciously points out, it is undeniable that in thinking it possible to exercise direct operational control from London over distant naval forces, the First Sea Lord was inviting just such a nemesis. Roskill concludes: "it is hard to justify such an intervention made in such a way."

We may easily understand now that despite Stalin's exhortations, when faced with these figures, Winston Churchill should have waited until September before permitting P.Q. 18 to set out. And even though it was provided with a powerful escort — including the escort carrier Avenger — 13 of the 40 vessels that then sailed from Hvalfjord were lost. But on the German side losses were not light: four submarines and 41 aircraft. The struggle in the Arctic waters was now draining the strength of both sides.

On September 14, weakened by the battles in the great curve of the Don, the 62nd Army had only 50,000 fighting men left. On the following night, however, a Regiment of the 13th Guards Division was sent hurriedly across the Volga in reinforcement and this enabled Lieutenant-General Chuikov to retake Matveyev-Kurgan hill. On September 17 more men, an infantry brigade and an armoured brigade, also crossed the river on ferries to take part in the defence of Stalingrad.

These reinforcements did not, however, prevent the German 6th Army, powerfully supported by Luftflotte IV, from scoring victories. By September 20 they had reached the banks of the Volga, slightly downstream of the station which they had finally occupied. This cut off the 62nd Army on its left from the 64th (Major-General M. S. Shumilov), and trapped it against the river for some 15 miles.

Factory to factory combat

This gave new impetus to the attack, whilst increased support was given by the Stukas of the Luftflotte's VIII Fliegerkorps. The Orlovka salient was reduced and then, on a front of only two and a half miles, the 94th and 389th infantry, the 100th Jäger and the 14th and 24th Panzer Divisions hurled themselves on to the great industrial complexes known as the "Dzerzinsky" and the "Barricades" on October 14.

From the opposing side, Major Grams offers us confirmation of the terrible battles of October, in which he took part as commander of a motorised battalion in the 14th Panzer Division. In his history of this famous unit he writes: "It was an appalling and exhausting battle at both ground level and underground in the ruins, the cellars, the drains of this large city. Man to man, hero to hero. Our tanks clambered over great mountains of rubble and plaster, their tracks screeching as they drove their way through ruined workshops, opening fire at point-blank range in narrow streets blocked by fallen masonry or in the narrow factory yards. Several of our armoured colossi shook visibly or blew up as they ran over mines."

The worst thing for the Germans to bear, according to Grams, was the fact that every night hundreds of ferries brought in reinforcements across the Volga and there was no way of stopping them. In fact, during the night of October 16–17, the

German troops in Stalingrad.

Soviet 138th Division (Colonel I. I. Lyudnikov) arrived at a very opportune moment to bolster up the defence of the "Barricades" factory sector. LI Corps under General von Seydlitz had occupied the Tractor Factory itself, and had even reached the river bank but, faced with the Russians' continuous and insurmountable resistance, their attacks petered out, as previous ones had done.

Meanwhile Hitler, who was in Munich to celebrate the eighteenth anniversary of the abortive 1923 Putsch among the faithful, considered the battle for Stalingrad, and with it the war in Russia, as won. "I wished," he shouted in his raucous voice, "to get to the Volga and at a certain time and a certain place. It happens to be named after Stalin himself. But do not think that that is why I directed our efforts against it; it could have had quite a different name. No. It is because this is a particularly important place. This is where 30 million tons of traffic comes to be sorted out, including some nine million tons of petrol. This is where all the cereals from the huge regions of the Ukraine and the Kuban' pass through on their way to the north. This is where manganese ore is sent. This is where there are huge trans-shipment facilities. I wanted to take it and let me tell you, for we are modest, we have it!" This message had more effect on the party members crowded into the Munich Beer Cellar than on the fighters on the Stalingrad front. They knew what the real truth was, and it was them Hitler now told to "finish it off". It also shows that the Führer did not know-or pretended not to know-about the railway linking Astrakhan' and Saratov, bypassing Stalingrad and the Volga's great western bend.

More German advances

Yet on November 11, the German LI Corps, still fighting in the breach, renewed its assaults with armour and sappers; at the cost of incredible effort it succeeded in isolating from the rest of the Russian 62nd Army the defenders of the "Barricades", whose courage still remained steadfast, and in overrunning the workers' quarters attached to the "Red October" factory. They got inside the factory itself, but then the attack ground to a halt. The 6th Army had worn itself out: its infantry companies were down to 80 or even 60 men, and the three divisions of its XIV Panzer Corps had only 199 tanks left of which many were inferior Czech types. The situation on the other side had also worsened considerably. On the west bank of the Volga the Russian 62nd Army only had 300 to 1,000 yards behind it. The river was beginning to bring down icefloes large enough to prevent supplies or reinforcements from crossing. The fact still remains, however, that by now Chuikov knew secretly that he had won a sufficient margin of time, albeit a small one, for Russia, and that within ten days or so the enemy would have something else to think about.

Some of the famous units of the Red Army which distinguished themselves in the defence of Stalingrad have already been mentioned. To these must also be added the 112th and the 308th Divisions, commanded respectively by Colonels I. Zh. Ermolkin and L. N. Gurtiev. Mindful of the soldier in the front line, we quote the tribute to this gigantic struggle by Marshal Eremenko, then in command of the Stalingrad Front.

"The epic of Stalingrad brought out particularly the high and noble qualities of the Soviet people and their heroic army:

German troops on the Eastern Front, with a MG34 machine gun.t

fervent patriotism, devotion to the Communist cause, fighting comradeship between soldiers of all nationalities, inflexible courage and self-sacrifice, unshakable firmness in defence, forceful bravery in attack, constant liaison and unfailing help between the front and rear areas, brotherhood between soldiers and workers in the factories and the fields. The heroic spirit which has breathed over Stalingrad has borne illustrious testimony to the power of the great Communist Party to guide and inspire our lives and to adapt itself to every circumstance, trustee as it is of the eternal ideas of Lenin."

It will be recalled that Hitler had assumed direct command of Army Group "A" in the Caucasus on September 10. Reduced to some 20 divisions since the transfer of the 4th Panzerarmee to Army Group "B", the Germans ended up in late autumn by failing at their last objectives also, just as Stalin had forecast to Winston Churchill. In the Black Sea area, autumn was drawing in and Gruppe Ruoff had not got beyond the foothills of the Caucasus. It was thus unable to complete that encircling movement which the Führer had calculated would have given him at best the ports of Tuapse and Sukhumi. The defenders were helped by the forests, the altitude, the rain, and then the snow, all of which showed up the lack of training of the German mountain troops who, however, had been driven very hard. Colonel-General von Kleist had reached Prokhladny on the River Terek, which flows out into the Caspian, on August 27. He was no luckier than the others. Held some 50 miles from the Grozny oilfields, he rallied his III Panzer Corps (General von Mackensen) and swung his attack upstream. This seems to have caught the defence by surprise and he took Nal'chik on October 25 and Alagir on November 5 but failed at Orzhonikidze as he was crossing the Terek. Worse still, this finger that he had rashly thrust into the enemy's positions was all but cut off in counter-attacks, and he nearly lost his 13th Panzer Division. Though it escaped, its near loss put an end to the 1st Panzerarmee's offensive for good and all.

The North Caucasus and the Trans-Caucasus Fronts were now being reinforced week by week, so that on about November 15 the 22 Axis divisions (15 German, 6 Rumanian, and one Slovak) were opposed by almost 90 major formations, including 37 infantry and eight or nine cavalry divisions, and eight armoured brigades. The tide was about to turn on Germany's effort to secure Caucasian oil.

The Soviet comeback

During their conversations in August, Stalin had told Winston Churchill that he intended to launch a great offensive as winter approached. So during the first fortnight in September Colonel-General A. M. Vasilevskii, replacing the sick Marshal Shaposhnikov as Chief-of-Staff, and his colleague General N. N. Voronov, head of the Red Army's artillery, were sent to the banks of the Volga to deal with the situation. When they returned to Stavka it was decided that the forthcoming operation should be in the hands of General G. K. Zhukov. It was expected to engage several Fronts or army groups. Colonel-General Eremenko then had to be relieved of some of his large command, on the South-East and Stalingrad Fronts. The former was renamed the Stalingrad Front and remained under his control; the second became the Don Front, under the command of Lieutenant-General K. K. Rokossovsky.

By the beginning of September 1942 the Soviet Supreme Command saw that the German reserves were becoming exhausted. They knew that the time had come when they could launch a major counterattack against their opponents.

Zhukov and Vasilevsky discussed these questions with Stavka, and they went to the Volga Front to judge the situation for themselves before drawing up a plan for a counter-offensive against the Axis forces. They were told to keep the purpose of their visit secret. At Stalingrad Zhukov ascertained the 6th Army's strength and calculated the numbers of men, tanks and guns the Russians would require for a successful offensive. He also reconnoitred the bridgeheads held by the Russian forces to the south of the River Don at Kletskaya and Serafimovich. Vasilevsky went to the south of Stalingrad to see sectors of the front held by the Russian 51st and 57th Armies between Krasnoarmeysk and Lake Barmantsak. On their return to Moscow Stavka invited the General Staff's Operations Directorate to help them to work out the details of a practical plan. Stavka took a direct control of the two new fronts (Stalingrad and Don) which were to conduct the counter-attack. By the end of the month they approved the plan and the General Staff were engaged in working out the operational details. Vasilevsky commanded the Stalingrad Front and Zhukov was given charge of the Don Front and the newly created South-West Front. The attack was to consist of a concentric movement north and south of Stalingrad against the thinly held flanks of the 6th Army, the Rumanian 3rd and 4th Armies and the underequipped 4th Panzer Army. The attack would then link up to the west of Stalingrad, thus trapping the 6th Army and destroying it. By the second half of October these plans were complete. The attack would take place on a front of 250 miles.

The Russian forces move up

When these decisions had been taken, the next step was to transport men and matériel to their concentration areas. The 5th Tank Army (Lieutenant-General P. L. Romanenko) was recalled from the Bryansk Front to become the spearhead of Vatutin's attack. IV Mechanised Corps (Major-General A. G. Kravchenko) and XIII Mechanised Corps (Major-General Tanichikhin) occupied the lake area south of Stalingrad under strict camouflage

Soviet soldiers advancing through the rubble of Stalingrad.

precautions as part of Eremenko's front.

In view of the decisive result expected from the campaign, Stavka did not hesitate to call upon half its reserve of artillery. Vatutin, Rokossovsky, and Eremenko thus got an additional 75 artillery regiments, bringing their total up to 230, or 13,540 guns and mortars. They were also sent 115 Katyusha batteries, with a total of 10,000 launchers. Two air armies were sent to the South-West Front and one each to the Don and Stalingrad Fronts, so that the three fronts had a total of 1,000 planes, including 600 fighters, to call on. This weight of equipment was to batter a hole in the thinly-held German fronts.

These troop and equipment movements were usually carried out at night and the strictest orders were given to preserve secrecy. This was also secured by manoeuvres designed to deceive the enemy. Radio operators on the Bryansk Front, for instance, continued to transmit messages for the benefit of enemy listening-posts long after the troops had left the area, and did not rejoin their units on the Don Front until the very last moment.

Can we conclude with Marshal Eremenko that if the German Supreme Command admitted the likelihood of a Russian counter-attack, "it still did not know precisely where or when it would take place"? Eremenko was no doubt basing his opinion on the authority of Colonel-General Jodl, who is said to have declared after the capitulation of the Third Reich: "We had no idea of the gigantic concentrations of Russian forces on the flank of the 6th Army. We did not know in what strength the Soviet troops were massing in this sector. Shortly before the attacks, there was nothing there and suddenly we were struck a massive blow, a blow which was to have far-reaching, even fatal, consequences."

We should remember, however, that at O.K.W. Jodl enjoyed only a partial view of the Eastern Front. From mid-October, both in the German 6th Army and the Rumanian 3rd Army, there was constant concern about enemy activity in the bridgeheads he controlled and on the right bank of the Don in the areas of Kletskaya and Serafimovich. Similar signs of movement had been noticed in the sector of the 4th Panzerarmee, which extended the right flank of the 6th Army, and Colonel-General Paulus deduced that the enemy was preparing some pincer movement which would be all the more dangerous for the Germans as the Rumanians on the flank were very poorly equipped with anti-tank weapons. He therefore strengthened his left flank by bringing over the Don the armoured unit of his 14th Panzer Division into General Strecker's XI Corps, but he could do no more as he had the strictest orders from Hitler to hold Stalingrad at all costs.

The satellites' part

Even before the start of the battle which was to bring about the final destruction of his army group, Colonel-General von Weichs was not optimistic about the outcome after the adverse reports of his Intelligence units. On the preceding October 10, the Rumanian 3rd Army (General Dumitrescu) had taken up positions between the left flank of the German 6th Army and the right flank of the Italian 8th Army (General Gariboldi). This was in execution of the directive of April 5, which laid down that the Don front should be defended by the satellite powers.

But between the right flank of the Rumanian 3rd Army, which adjoined the left flank of the German 6th Army, and the left flank of the Hungarian 2nd Army (Colonel-General Jany) which adjoined the German 2nd Army, the Don front was some 310 miles long. The three satellite armies which were being asked to defend it had between them some 30 divisions. All of them were somewhat weak in infantry, lacking in mobility and, especially, very badly equipped both qualitatively and quantitatively to meet armour ed attack. The Rumanian 3rd Army was particularly badly situated as it faced the two bridgeheads at Kletskaya and Serafimovich, where the Russians had held out in the previous summer against all attacks and, without being able to take advantage of the river obstacle, the Rumanian battalions each had an average front of over three miles.

Marshal Antonescu, the Rumanian dictator, had not failed to draw Hitler's attention to the extreme danger of the situation. In particular he had asked Hitler for 5-cm anti-tank guns to replace the earlier 3.7-cm weapons with which the Rumanians were equipped and which were recognised as completely obsolete. The Führer had promised to supply these without delay, but his promise remained empty words and a catastrophe became inevitable. Army Group "B" was thus in a position of "pre-rupture".

The position was further blackened by the fact that the strategic reserves available to Weichs consisted of only four divisions, two German infantry divisions, and the two armoured divisions of the XLVIII Panzer Corps. One of these two, however, the Rumanian 1st Armoured Division (Radu) had never been in action, and both were under strength.

Soviet snipers in Stalingrad.

The operation, under Zhukov's overall command, had been baptised "Uranus" in Moscow and was launched in two phases.

At 0730 hours on November 19, after a general rocket barrage the artillery of the South-West and the Don Fronts opened Sap. on the German-Rumanian positions north-west of Stalingrad with about 90 guns per mile of Front. According to the Russians, the density of this concentration was made less effective because of thick fog. Be that as it may, the entire telephone network of the Rumanian 3rd Army was put out of action as the wires were cut by the shelling. The fog also helped the surprise effect. At 0848 the Soviet barrage moved forward, and infantry and tanks flung themselves into the assault.

On the South-West Front, the 5th Tank Army (Lieutenant-General P. L. Romanenko) had as its task the annihilation of the Rumanian defence facing the Serafimovich bridgehead, but it met such resistance that its commander had to use up in the breakthrough some of the tanks he had planned to hold back for exploitation of the breach. But then the defence collapsed. At nightfall, two Soviet tank corps, protected on their flanks by corps of cavalry, broke through the breach and poured into the enemy's rear, causing fearful panic.

Further to the east, the Soviet 21st Army broke out of the Kletskaya bridgehead on a front of nearly nine miles. Under the command of Major-General I. M. Chistyakov, it also had to use its armoured forces to overcome the resistance of the Rumanians. By the end of the day it had had the same success as the 5th Tank Army. The Rumanian V Armoured Corps (General M. Lascar), which was holding out between Kletskaya and Serafimovich, saw that it was doomed to encirclement.

On the Don Front, the Soviet 65th Army (Lieutenant-General P. I. Batov), attacking from the Kletskaya bridgehead towards Vertyachiy, where the Germans had bridged the Don, was caught at a disadvantage in deep ravines. It also ran up against the XI Corps, which formed the left flank of the 6th Army, and was counterattacked furiously by the 14th Panzer Division. It was therefore able to make only modest advances. The 24th Army (Major-General I. Galanin), which had been ordered to advance along the left bank of the Don, was similarly held up. The 66th Army (Lieutenant-General A. S. Zhadov) was to make a diversion

76mm Soviet field gun.

in the Don-Volga isthmus, stubbornly defended by the VIII Corps (General W. Heitz).

On the Axis side, the XLVIII Panzer Corps, on stand-by since dawn, rumbled off at 0930 hours towards Kletskaya, where it was thought that the main Russian effort was being made, with orders to engage it without worrying about the flanks. Towards 1100 hours, in the light of new information, General Heim was ordered to drive towards Serafimovich — a switch from north-east to north-west. In the fog this counter-order produced confusion, contact was lost, and both the 22nd Panzer Division (Major-General Rodt) and the Rumanian 1st Armoured Division ran blindly into the Soviet 5th Tank Army. In the evening Heim was surrounded and his troops were in a very bad way.

On November 20, to the south-west of Stalingrad, the second phase of the Soviet offensive opened under Colonel-General Eremenko, from a line Lake Tastsa-Lake Sarpa-Krasnoarmeysk, with the 64th, 57th, and 51st Armies under the command respectively of Major-Generals M. S. Shumilov, F. I. Tolbukhin and N. I. Trufanov. To exploit the expected breakthrough, Eremenko had put the XIII Mechanised Corps (Major-General T. I. Tanichikhin) under 57th Army, whilst the 51st Army had been given the IV Mechanised Corps and the IV Cavalry Corps (Major-Generals V. T. Volsky and T. T. Shapkin). On the other side, all Colonel-General Hoth had left of his former Panzerarmee was IV Corps (General E. Jaenecke), but he did have the Rumanian 4th Army, of which General C. A. Constantinescu was about to take over the command. He thus had seven infantry divisions (two of which were German), and two Rumanian

cavalry divisions. He held in reserve the excellent 29th Motorised Division.

Delayed by fog, the attack started at 1000 hours, but by early afternoon the breakthrough had come in the sector of the Rumanian VI Corps whose 1st, 2nd, and 18th Divisions were virtually wiped out. The 29th Motorised Division tried to restore the situation and scored some early victories. But as the only unit capable of counter-attacking amidst the general rout, it soon had to abandon the positions it had won for fear of being surrounded. Eremenko was not long in letting loose his cavalry and mechanised units, and on the following day, at 1030 hours, IV Cavalry Corps galloped into the village of Abganerovo, a station

German 8.8cm Flak.

Red Army approach German strong point North West of Stalingrad.

staff of the Rumanian II Corps was so taken by surprise that when the patrols of the XXVI Tank Corps (Major-General A. G. Rodin) reached their headquarters they found tables laden with maps and documents, cupboards open, keys in the locks of chests, teleprinters still connected, and officers' caps still hanging on their pegs. XLVIII Panzer Corps, as a result of a breakdown in radio communications, was out of touch with the Rumanian 1st Armoured Division, but managed to break out of the encirclement. In the evening of November 20 it would have obeyed Weichs' order to retreat had it not had, through a Führerbefehl, the overriding order to extricate the Rumanian V Corps. This was an impossible task, and once again XLVIII Corps was surrounded. Yet it finally managed to reach the German lines, though at the cost of its 22nd Panzer Division, which was reduced virtually to scrap.

The day of November 22 had not yet dawned before destiny had given her verdict. The night before, the Soviet XXVI Tank Corps, forming General Romanenko's left-hand column, was within striking distance of Kalach after covering over 62 miles in three days. The disorder had to be exploited at once and so General Rodin decided to take the bridge over the Don by surprise. He put under the command of Colonel Philippov of the 14th Motorised Brigade a detachment of two infantry companies. They were to advance behind five captured and restored German tanks each carrying 12 men armed with submachine guns. Rumbling forward with all their lights on, as the Germans did, Philippov's detachment overwhelmed the bridge guard then drove off the German counter-attacks. The defence was further confused

on the Stalingrad–Novorossiysk railway line. A few minutes later Nikita Khruschev was on the scene, bringing congratulations and encouragement.

In the great sweep of the Don on this same November 20, Vatutin and Rokossovsky energetically exploited their successes of the day before. The former used his 5th Tank Army and the latter his IV Tank Corps (Major-General G. P. Kravchenko) and his III Guards Corps (Major-General I. A. Pliev). Meanwhile the 21st Army completed the encirclement of the Rumanian V Corps, which then turned south and fought with some tenacity.

But how could it face an attack by some 900 tanks and two cavalry corps? At dawn on November 20, at Perelazovskiy, the by the shooting-match going on at the same time between the tanks of the 6th Army and those of the Soviets.

Meanwhile Eremenko had eagerly exploited his victory of November 20. Driving his IV Cavalry Corps along the railway from Kuban', he moved his IV Mechanised Corps north-west until at 1030 hours on November 23 it linked up with the IV Tank Corps from the Don Front in the village of Sovetskiy some 18–19 miles south east of Kalach. This completed the encirclement of the Axis troops in the Stalingrad area. The following day Khruschev came in person to congratulate Generals Volsky and Kravchenko and to enquire about the needs of the troops. This same day (November 24) saw the end of all Rumanian resistance in the Don pockets. The previous evening General Lascar, who had just been awarded the Iron Cross with Oak Leaves by Hitler, had had to surrender through lack of ammunition. On the 24th General Stenesco did the same and 33,000 Rumanians took the road to captivity.

Göring's responsibility

Shaken by the forceful argument of Gen eral Zeitzler, Hitler had been restored to vigour by the assurances of Reichsmarschall Göring. These were received in silence by Colonel-General Jeschonnek but had the support of Field-Marshal Keitel and Colonel-General Jodl. The 6th Army reckoned that it needed 700 tons of supplies a day. This meant the necessary food, animal fodder, petrol, and ammunition to keep going, albeit at a reduced rate, 250,000 men, 8,000 horses, 1,800 guns, and 10,000 vehicles. With a carelessness that can only be called criminal,

German soldier looking at enemy positions through a periscope.

Göring undertook to assure them of 500 tons a day. He based this on the successful supply of the far smaller pockets at Kholm and Demyansk where, for five months from January 1942, 100,000 Germans had held out thanks to supplies from the air.

Indeed, as Colonel-General von Richthofen, the man on the spot, had predicted from the outset, the supplying of the 6th Army by air was a complete and disastrous failure. In actual fact, from December 1 to 12 deliveries to the Stalingrad pocket amounted to an average of 97.3 tons of petrol and ammunition a day. From December 13 to 31 this increased by some 40 tons, then fell again as a consequence of the progressive deterioration of the strategic position and the weather. The average over the whole 70 days of the airlift was 91.16 tons a day, so that Göring's shortfall may be reckoned at 81 per cent. The loss of 488 planes, including 266 Junkers Ju 52's and 1,000 aircrew must also be included on the debit side. On the credit side, 25,000 sick and wounded were evacuated.

In the Stalingrad pocket, to which Paulus had transferred his headquarters, the Führerbefehl of November 23 had been the object of bitter argument at the highest level. General von Seydlitz (LI Corps) held that it should be ignored as Hitler did not know the realities of the situation, and that a breakout should be attempted along the line of the railway to Kuban'. Major-General Arthur Schmidt, chief-of-staff of the 6th Army, held the opposite view, both out of respect for orders and because he reckoned that the movement advised by the commander of LI Corps would end in catastrophe compounded by a complete breakdown of discipline. Paulus, though feeling little conviction, decided that his chief-of-staff was right. The German 6th Army thus dug itself into a pocket measuring some 37 miles between Stalingrad and its western perimeter and 25 miles from north to south. The day after the breakthrough at Lake Tsatsa, IV Corps had come under 6th Army command, though XI Corps, as it retreated across the Don after the surprise attack at Kalach, had taken with it the Rumanian 1st Cavalry Division. Paulus thus commanded five corps, in all 15 infantry divisions, three motorised divisions, three Panzer divisions, and one division of cavalry. These totalled some 278,000 men including the units left outside the pocket.

Manstein's new task

Hitler entrusted the mission of freeing the beleaguered troops in Stalingrad to Field-Marshal Erich von Manstein.

A few days after his victory at Sevastopol', the new Field-Marshal, with four divisions of his 11th Army and the great guns which had demolished the Soviets' emplacements, was transferred to Army Group "North" for, in spite of Halder's objections, Hitler had decided to seize Leningrad without waiting for a solution on the Stalingrad front. This offensive, called "Nordlicht", never got started, as the Russians moved first and the 11th Army found itself from August 27 to October 2 using up its strength to bolster up a weakened 18th Army, which had given way, and then having to iron out the salients knocked into the front.

On November 21, when he was in Vitebsk, Manstein received the order to take over forthwith the command of a new army group, Army Group "Don", which would contain the 6th Army, Gruppen Hoth and Hollidt, and the Rumanian 3rd Army. Its task was defined as follows: "To arrest the enemy's attacks and to regain the ground lost since the beginning of his offensive."

On the 24th he was at the headquarters of Army Group "B", now reduced to the Italian 8th Army, the Hungarian 2nd Army, and the German 2nd Army. Colonel-General von Weichs informed him of the state in which he would find the units allotted to him. Now cut off, the German 6th Army had lost all freedom of movement. Along the line Stalingrad — Novorossiysk, Gruppe Hoth was, if the phrase may be permitted, no more than a strategic expression. Having lost its IV Corps and its 16th Motorised Division, immobilised on the Kalmuk Steppe by the

Soviet soldiers advance along a railway track in a Stalingrad suburb.

camels and recruited in Central Asia. Naturally enough, it was virtually wiped out.

Yet it was not before December 10 that the 4th Panzerarmee, part of Gruppe Hoth, was able to go over to the offensive. It was in fact reduced to nothing more than LVII Panzer Corps (General F. Kirchner), as the Rumanian VI and VII Corps could not be relied on. The 6th Panzer Division was soon up to its full strength with 160 tanks, a battalion of half-tracks, and 42 self-propelled guns. Not so the 23rd Panzer Division (Lieutenant-General von Boineburg-Lengsfeld) hurriedly brought up from the Caucasus, which went into action with only 20 tanks. These figures are important in view of the claims of Soviet historians that Manstein went into action in what they pompously call his "counter-offensive" with 460 armoured vehicles.

On December 12–13, LVII Panzer Corps nevertheless forced a crossing of the Aksay in spite of resistance from the Russian 51st Army of the Stalingrad Front. The valiant Eremenko thought this serious enough to appeal to Supreme Headquarters. "I reported it to J. V. Stalin," he wrote. "Alarmed by this information he sent a message 'Hold out. We will send you reserves immediately.' And he added 'Supreme Headquarters has finally realised what danger you were in.' The situation was becoming very serious: the reserves might be too late." This was why he threw in his XIII and IV Mechanised Corps, in spite of their being worn out. They counter-attacked furiously whilst the Germans put in their 17th Panzer Division, which had only 30 tanks, from the Orel front. The Panzer division's commander, Major-General F. von Senger and Etterlin signalled Hoth: "Situation regarding matériel

express order of Hitler, the 4th Panzerarmee was reduced to a handful of Rumanian divisions which had escaped the débâcle of November 20. In the great loop of the Don, General Hollidt somehow improvised a defensive line behind the Chir so as to deny to the enemy the defence of the main river.

On November 26 Field-Marshal von Manstein set up his headquarters at Novocherkassk. On the 27th, 78 trains from France arrived in Kotel'nikovo station, 100 miles south-west of Stalingrad, bringing in the first units of the 6th Panzer Division (Major-General E. Raus). These were greeted by artillery fire and began their career on the Eastern Front by driving off the Soviet IV Cavalry Corps. This included a brigade of troops mounted on very bad." Hoth replied: "Some divisions up front are even worse off. Yours has an excellent reputation. I am counting on you." The attacks started again and on December 15 Eremenko had to sound the alarm a second time. Stavka promised him the prompt aid of the 2nd Guards Army (Lieutenant-General R. Ya. Malinovsky). This army did, in fact, succeed in preventing Kirchner from breaking out of the bridgehead he had won on the north bank of the Myshkova. Hoth had thus won 50 miles in eight days and was within 30 miles of his objective. But he had worn out his men. Conscious of his subordinate's difficulties, Manstein planned to bring over the XLVIII Panzer Corps from the north to the south bank of the Don, which would allow him to take up again the advance towards Stalingrad, from which Paulus now said he could not break out through lack of fuel. But things turned out very differently.

Operation "Saturn"

On December 16, the Soviet High Command set in motion Operation "Saturn", intended as a pincer movement by the South-West and Voronezh Front (Lieutenant-General F. 1. Golikov) which was intended to destroy the Italian 8th Army and the Rumanian 3rd Army and open the way to Rostov. Co-ordination of the attack was entrusted to General Zhukov. The artillery preparation at dawn on D-day required the concentration of 5,000 guns and mortars. On the South-West Front the Russian 3rd Guards Army (Lieutenant-General D. D. Lelyushenko) soon overcame the resistance of the Rumanian 7th and 11th Divisions and forced the XVII Corps to abandon its positions. This done,

it exploited its success in the rear areas of the Italian 8th Army (General Gariboldi), whose 230,000 men in nine divisions were deployed on a front of 170 miles. And the Don was now frozen hard enough for tanks to cross. Not only that, but the catastrophe of November 19 had forced Hitler to withdraw its "stays" (the 62nd and 294th Divisions). It had only 380 47-mm guns to defend itself against the enemy tanks, but even twice this number would still have been unable to pierce the Russian armour. Finally, the Italians had only 55 tanks, and these were obsolete. So the army which the boastful Mussolini had flung defiantly at the Russians was now the mere shadow of a real force.

General Golikov had massed in the Verkhne Mamon bridgehead the 1st Guards Army (Lieutenant-General V. I. Kuznetsov) and the 6th Army (Lieutenant-General F. M. Kharitonov). Between them they had 15 infantry divisions supported by many tanks, which operated at battalion strength. Opposite them was the Italian II Corps, with the "Cossiera" and the "Ravenna" Divisions. In such conditions of inequality, the breakthrough took only 48 hours and on December 18 no fewer than five armoured corps poured through the breach which Colonel-General von Weichs was striving in vain to close. How could he have done this when his 27th Panzer Division had only 50 tanks?

At Novocherkassk the defeat of Army Group "B" forced Manstein not only to countermand the order to XLVIII Panzer Corps to go to the rescue of the LVII, but on December 23 to order Kirchner to pull the valiant 6th Panzer Division back across the Don. This latter was the only complete formation in the forces designated to free Paulus. It therefore meant that the whole enterprise had been abandoned; This was on a day when the temperature was 30 degrees centigrade below zero and the men's menu was:

Midday: rice and horsemeat.

Evening: 7 ounces of bread, two meatballs (horse) à la Stalingrad, ¾ ounce of butter and real coffee.

Extras: 4 ounces of bread, an ounce of boiled sweets, and 4 ounces of chocolate.

Tobacco: one cigar and two cigarettes.

The significance of this was conveyed by Paulus to a young major from Luftflotte IV attached to his staff. His words betray his emotion and despair: "We couldn't even pull in our outposts, as the men were falling down from exhaustion. They have had nothing to eat for four days. What can I reply, I an Army Commander, if a soldier comes up to me and says, 'Please, Colonel-General sir, a little bit of bread'? We have eaten the last horses. Could you ever imagine soldiers falling on a dead horse, cutting off its head, and devouring its brains raw? How can we go on fighting when the men haven't even got winter clothing? Who is the man who said we would be supplied by air?"

Kirchner was now down to his 17th and 23rd Panzer Divisions with less than 60 tanks between them. Could he hold the Myshkova line? It was unlikely now that the enemy had thrown in the 2nd Guards Army with its numerous powerful armoured formations. The order of December 23 was therefore a sentence of death on the German 6th Army. Also the loss of the aerodromes at Tatsinskaya and Morozovsk meant that their supplies had to travel an extra 125 miles.

Manstein could not avoid involvement in this disastrous state of affairs. If Vatutin and Golikov got to Rostov, it would not be only the 6th Army which would be wiped out, but the catastrophe would spread to what was left of Army Groups "Don" and "A". We can only conclude that a system of operations is doomed to destruction when it subjects the commanders to such a dilemma.

"In war, a great disaster always pins great guilt on one man" said Napoleon. In obedience to this dictum Hitler had the commander of the XLVIII Panzer Corps, Lieutenant-General Heim, dragged before a court-martial presided over by Göring. He was condemned to death. Secretly imprisoned in the Moabit Gaol in Berlin, he was released without a word of explanation in May 1943 then, the next year, although banished from the army,

Soviet soldiers fight in Red October tractor works.

On December 24, 1942, the South-West Front's offensive against Rostov forced the Luftwaffe formations which were supplying the Stalingrad pocket to make a hurried departure from their bases at Morozovsk and Tatsinskaya and establish a new base at Sal'sk, and obliged them to fly over 200, instead of 120, miles to carry out their missions. The retreat of the 4th Panzerarmee along the Stalingrad–Novorossiysk railway forced them to withdraw further on January 4, 1943. Now they had to take off from Shakhty and Novocherkassk, some 275 miles from the 6th Army's aerodromes. In this way the development of the strategic situation aggravated the consequences of the criminal irresponsibility with which Göring had boasted of being able to supply the so-called "fortress" at a rate of 500 tons a day. In fact there were only six days between January 4 and 21 during which the unfortunate forces of the besieged army received more than 100 tons of supplies.

The supplying of Stalingrad by air was therefore a failure and one of the most important causes of the surrender. This theme recurs constantly in Field-Marshal Paulus's notes: "You are in fact addressing yourself to men who are already dead", he wrote in answer to a suggestion that he make sorties. "We have stayed here on the orders of the Führer. The Air Force has left us in the lurch and has never kept its promises."

A decision was reached on three drop zones for parachuting supplies behind the divisional sectors, but Paulus objected: "If you insist on parachuting supplies, this army is finished. You must land because our most absolute need is for fuel."

Later, there is a diatribe against Göring: "At the same time I learn from Manstein and Zeitzler that, during a vital meeting, the Reichsmarschall said that re-supplying was not going so badly out there! … He has big boots so it wouldn't do him any harm to come here himself and see the situation! Clearly my reports have not been passed on to him or he has not taken them seriously. In the old days I should have made my decision at once but now they treat you like a naughty child and what else can you do but grin and bear it?"

The fate of Stalingrad sealed

On January 10, 1943, at 0805 hours, the entire artillery of the Don Front, grouped under the command of Lieutenant-General M. I. Kazakov, with more than 7,000 guns and mortars, opened a torrential fire on the positions of the 6th Army. At 0900 hours, the barrage started to creep forward, thus giving the Soviet 65th and 21st Armies (Lieutenant-General P. I. Batov and Major-General I. M. Chistyakov) the signal to attack. Within three days they had wiped out the Marinovka salient in concentric assaults. By January 17, unleashing his 24th and 57th Armies (Generals I. V. Galinin and F. I. Tolbukhin) on the left and the right, Rokossovsky, who had arrived at Voroponvo, had reconquered two-thirds of the pocket and, most importantly, had taken the aerodrome at Gumrak, the last one still left in German hands, thus preventing German aircraft from landing.

From then on, the remains of the 6th Army were supplied as far as possible by dropping containers. But the end was close, for the physical and moral resistance of the defenders was becoming rapidly exhausted and, at 1600 hours on January 22, Paulus

German Junkers flies in supplies for ground forces.

transmitted the following message to Hitler:

"After having repelled at the outset massive enemy attacks, wide and deep gaps torn in the lines of the XIV Panzer Corps and the IV Corps noon on 22. All ammunition has been exhausted. Russians advancing on both sides of Voroponvo on a 6-kilometre front. Flags waving here and there. No longer any chance of stemming the flood. Neighbouring fronts, also without any ammunition, contracting. Sharing ammunition with other fronts no longer feasible either. Food running out. More than 12,000 wounded in the pocket untended. What orders should I issue to troops who have no more ammunition and are under continuous attack from masses of artillery, tanks, and infantry? Immediate

reply essential as signs of collapse already evident in places. Yet confidence still maintained in the command."

Manstein pressed Hitler to answer this telegram, which hinted at surrender, by giving his permission to Paulus to lay down his arms. But three-quarters of an hour of telephoned appeals did not succeed in weakening the Führer's savage obstinacy. And so, on January 26, as the 21st Army exploited its success of January 22 by pushing eastward, it linked up on Mamaev-Kurgan hill with the Soviet 62nd Army (Lieutenant-General V. I. Chuikov) which had so bravely defended the ruins of Stalingrad. And thus the German pocket was split in two.

In the southern pocket, General von Hartmann, commander of the 71st Division, rashly exposed himself to fire and was killed'

German SS - Das Reich, Shurzen plates.

rifle in hand, while General Stempel of the 113th committed suicide. Their fellow commanders Drebber and Dimitriu surrendered the 297th Division and the Rumanian 20th Division; General von Seydlitz-Kurzbach, commander of the LI Corps, followed their example.

Paulus surrenders

Paulus, on whom, as the end approached, the Führer had conferred the supreme distinction of promotion to Field-Marshal, was by dawn on January 30 trapped in the basement of the large department store in

Stalingrad where he had set up his final headquarters. Together with his staff he accepted the inevitable. General M. S. Shumilov, commanding the Soviet 64th Army, gives the following account of his surrender:

"As our officers entered the room, Paulus was sitting on his bed. According to the accounts given by members of the Russian group, he gave the impression of a man in the last stages of exhaustion. The staff of the 6th Army was given one hour to move out. At that moment Major-General Laskin, Chief-of-Staff of the 64th Army, arrived, with my order to bring Paulus and Schmidt, his chief-of-staff, to 64th Army headquarters at Beketovka.

"A tall, wasted, greying man, in the uniform of a Colonel-General, entered the room. It was Paulus.

"Following the custom under the Hitler régime, he raised his arm as if he were about to give the regulation 'Heil Hitler' cry. But he stopped himself in time, lowered his arm, and wished us the usual German 'Guten Tag'.

"General Shumilov requested the prisoner to show his identity documents. Paulus took a wallet out of his pocket and handed the Soviet army commander his military paybook, the usual document carried by German officers. Mikhail Stepanovich looked at it and then asked for other identification confirming that Paulus was in fact the commander of the German 6th Army. Holding these documents, he then asked if it was true that Paulus had been promoted Generalfeldmarschall. General Schmidt declared:

"'By order of the Führer, the Colonel-General was promoted yesterday to the highest rank in the Reich, Generalfeldmarschall.'

"'Then can I tell our Supreme Command Headquarters that Generalfeldmarschall Paulus has been taken prisoner by troops of my army?' insisted Shumilov, addressing himself to Paulus.

'Jawohl,' came the reply, which needs no translation."

All the same, the northern pocket continued to hold out until February 2, and General Strecker, commanding the XI Corps, was the last to surrender.

The toll

The cold facts of the matter were that the Russians buried 147,200 German and Rumanian dead in the Stalingrad pocket, while they themselves suffered 46,700 dead, according to Marshal Eremenko. These figures illustrate the savagery of that final battle. The five corps and the 22 divisions (two Rumanian)

which perished left in Russian hands slightly more than 91,000 prisoners, including 24 generals and 2,500 officers, as well as more than 6,000 guns and 60,000 motor vehicles. The only troops to escape the trap by being flown out were 24,000 sick and wounded and 18,000 specialists or high-ranking officers marked down for promotion. Of the 91,000 prisoners, very few were still alive in 1950.

After the surrender, the Russians celebrated their victory. Recalling the moment, Marshal Eremenko recounts the following story:

"During the evening, at the very modest dinner to which the city council entertained us, General Shumilov, commander of the 64th Army, whose units had taken Field-Marshal Paulus prisoner together with his Staff, handed the German's personal weapon over to Nikita Sergeivich [Khruschev], saying: 'The weapon of the defeated Field-Marshal belongs by right to the commander of the Stalingrad Front, which has taken all the weight of the Nazi attack and also an important part in our counter-offensive.'

"Nikita Sergeivich came to see me on his way back to the front headquarters. I was in bed, with constant and cramping leg pains. Comrade Khruschev gave me an account of his day and then handed me a small burnished metal revolver: 'It's Field-Marshal Paulus's personal weapon. The Commander of the 64th Army hands it over to the commander of the Stalingrad Front, now happily no longer in existence. I consider that it is yours by right, Andrei Ivanovich.'

"So I took the pistol gratefully, as a symbol of the unforgettable days of the great battle."

The Russians move on

As described above, the defeat of the Rumanian 3rd Army and the Italian 8th Army in the great bend of the Don had forced Gruppe "Hoth", which was moving towards the pocket, to suspend its offensive on the evening of December 23, 1942. Already extremely weakened, it was thrown back by Colonel-General Eremenko, who had just been opportunely reinforced by the 2nd Guards Tank Army (Lieutenant-General R. Ya. Malinovsky.) On December 29, Hoth lost Kotel'nikovo, two days later Elista, on the Kalmuk Steppe, and, on January 2, moved back behind the Tsimlyansk–Remontnoye line. Of course, in the battles themselves Hoth had not lost the 571 tanks that the special Moscow communiqué claimed he had, for he had never more than 200 under his command. All the same, the troops of the Russian South Front now saw the road to Rostov open to them. The South Front had replaced the Stalingrad Front on January 2, under the same commander, Eremenko.

German disorder

Manstein had his work cut out trying to prevent the armies of the South-West Front (Lieutenant-General N. F. Vatutin) from engulfing Gruppe "Hollidt" and crossing the Donets near Kamensk-Shakhtinskiy and Voroshilovgrad, which would have opened the way dangerously towards Taganrog. So the defeat of Army Group "B" burst upon him like a thunderbolt in his headquarters at Stalino.

Overall command of this third act of the Soviet winter offensive had been entrusted to Lieutenant-General F. I. Golikov, commanding the Voronezh Front. His left wing, positioned in the region of Kantemirovka, faced the Italian Alpine Corps, and his right, to the north-west of Voronezh, was in contact with the German 2nd Army (Colonel-General von Salmuth.) On December 20, 1942 Golikov received orders from Stavka to crush the enemy forces between Kantemirovka and Voronezh, principally the Hungarian 2nd Army under Colonel-General Jany.

For this purpose, Golikov divided his forces into three main attack groups. On his left, the 3rd Tank Army (Lieutenant-General P. S. Rybalko) would move out from a line stretching from Kantemirovka to Novaya Kalitva and push in a north-westerly direction towards Alekseyevka; there it would make contact with the 40th Army of Major-General K. S. Moskalenko, which in its turn would move off from the bridgehead that the Russians had kept at Storogevoye on the right bank of the Don, 100 miles south of Voronezh. In that way the Hungarian 2nd Army would be caught in a pincer while, by using the bridgehead at Bobrov, the XVIII Corps (Major-General Sykov) would attack in the centre and try to cut through the enemy's rear and meet Rybalko's right wing. Although it is true, as the Great Patriotic War states, that the attacking forces had superiority only in artillery and armour, their superiority in these two arms must have been considerable.

With two armoured corps and eight armoured brigades, Golikov must have had about 900 tanks to face the 19th and 27th Panzer Divisions and the Hungarian 1st Armoured Division (15 tanks). As for the artillery, it should be noted that when the Russian 40th Army moved out of the Storogevoye bridgehead, its advance was heralded by a barrage laid down by 750 guns and howitzers and 672 mortars, in other words by 179 guns per mile. Furthermore, one-fifth of the Russian artillery, including medium calibre 122-mm and 152-mm guns, fired directly at enemy positions which had been pinpointed for a long time. On January 13, after a ferocious two-hour bombardment, the armour of the Soviet 3rd Tank Army was seen to move forward, 48 vehicles to each mile of front. Success was total. Not only did the Hungarian 2nd Army disintegrate under the powerful thrust, but the XXIV Panzer Corps and the Italian Alpine Corps, on the right, were also swept away in the defeat. As a result, by January 19 Rybalko's tanks were already close to Valuyki on the Oskol, 75 miles from their jumping-off point. In addition, the Hungarian rout endangered the German 2nd Army, which was positioned between the Don above Voronezh and the region north of Kursk, linking Army Group "B" with Army Group "Centre" (Field-Marshal von Kluge). To sum up, the break-up of the German front had taken place in a few days over a front of more than 215 miles from Livny to Kantemirovka, while Manstein had no firm positions left on the Donets above Voroshilovgrad.

Russian exploitation

At that moment, Colonel-General A. M. Vasilevsky, who had overall command of the Voronezh and South-West Fronts, slipped the leash on his two subordinate commanders. Golikov crashed through the remains of Army Group "B" while Vatutin, on his left, received orders to attack Army Group "Don" across the Donets. Golikov moved swiftly west and south-

west and, on February 8, his 60th Army (Major-General I. D. Chernyakhovsky) took Kursk, which had been held against all attacks the previous winter, while his 40th Army moved through Belgorod and Volchansk, and his 3rd Tank Army, further to the south, described a pincer movement which would give it Khar'kov. Vatutin, passing through Kupyansk, reached the Donets on February 7, crossed it the following day at Izyum and Balakleya, and fanned out south of the river. All in all, the style of campaign of May 12, 1942 was being repeated, but with better chances of success than the previous year for, on one hand, the German armies had been bled white and on the other, the Russian forces of the South-West Front had Manstein in a trap, both on the Mius front and on the Donets at Voroshilovgrad. In those circumstances, Stalin thought that, on February 6, he could safely order the South-West Front to "Seize Sinel'nikovo with the 6th Army and then, with all speed, Zaporozh'ye, so as to cut the enemy off from all possibility of retreat on the west bank of the Dniepr over the bridges at Dniepropetrovsk and Zaporozh'ye."

In the same tone an order was dispatched to the Voronezh Front to press energetically on to Poltava so as to reach the Dniepr near Kremenchug. But, as the Great Patriotic War correctly points out, this ukase took no account of the losses suffered by Golikov and Vatutin during six weeks of attacks which had taken them 200 and 240 miles respectively from their supply bases. Some armoured brigades, for example, had been reduced to six tanks and some infantry battalions to 20odd men. Even the better off units were absolutely exhausted.

Manstein's successes

Army Group "South" unleashed a counteroffensive on February 21. In this it broke the rule which seemed, in the judgement of the most prudent, to sum up the experience of 1918: contain, and only then counterattack. It is true that there were insufficient numbers of infantry available for containment and that Manstein had command of 13 divisions of armour or of Panzergrenadiers, in all about 800 tanks, including a considerable number of Pzkw VI Tigers. But the Russians misunderstood the reshuffling of Manstein's forces. This is how the Great Patriotic War describes the situation:

"Both the South-West Front command and Soviet Supreme Command were led to believe from the enemy's retreat from the lower Donets to the Mius and the transfer of his armoured and motorised divisions from around Rostov to near Konstantinovka, that the Germans intended to evacuate the Donets basin and retire behind the Dniepr. That is why Supreme Headquarters kept to its decision to develop its attack as soon as possible."

The result of this error of judgement and of the German initiative was a series of battles and clashes in which the clumsier Russians did not come off best.

On February 22, attacking due south from Krasnograd, the S.S. I Panzer Corps (1st "Leibstandarte" Panzergrenadier Division and 2nd "Das Reich" Panzergrenadier Division) crushed the Russian forces attacking Novomoskovsk as they advanced; then, reinforced by the 3rd "Totenkopf" Panzergrenadier Division of the Waffen S.S., the corps pushed on hard towards Pavlograd where it came under the 4th Panzerarmee, which Manstein

was pushing towards Lozovaya at the same speed. During these strategic moves, Lieutenant-General M. M. Popov's armoured force was utterly destroyed and, with its defeat, the entire South-West Front behind the Donets was forced into flight.

Khar'kov retaken

Though this retreat was justified in the circumstances (General Vatutin had lost 32,000 killed and captured, 615 tanks, and 423 guns), it nevertheless exposed the left wing of the Voronezh Front, which was now threatened halfway between Khar' kov and Poltava. On March 5, the 4th Panzerarmee hit the Soviet 3rd Tank Army hard near Krasnograd. Then a pincer attack enabled the S.S. I Panzer Corps to "lay Khar'kov at the feet of the Führer" on March 14, 1943. Gruppe "Kempf", fighting to the north of the city, drove forward at the same time and, on March 18, its Panzergrenadier division, the "Grossdeutschland", reoccupied Belgorod.

The III and XL Panzer Corps of the 1st Panzerarmee mopped up the Debal'tsevo, Makeyevka, and Kramatorskaya pockets. The result of this drive was that the VII Guards Cavalry Corps (Major-General Borisov), the IV Guards Mechanised Corps (Major-General Tanichikhin), and the XXV Tank Corps (Major-General Pavlov) found themselves trapped and then surrounded. The bridgehead at Matveyev-Kurgan, on the west bank of the Mius, was retaken by the 6th Army.

The spring thaw

About March 18, the thaw and the resultant mud caused operations to come to a halt between Kursk and the Sea of Azov. On that day, an O.K.W. communiqué proclaimed that Manstein's counter-attack had cost the enemy more than 50,000 killed, 19,594 prisoners, 3,000 guns, and 1,410 tanks. Without even questioning the figures, it is easy to put them into proportion by revealing that, in contrast, the Red Army had destroyed between 40 and 45 German and satellite divisions — a quarter of the forces the Russians had before them — in four months.

Soviet tanks on outskirts of city KV-1 heavy tanks.

Russian troops on the move.

Operation "Zitadelle" was launched on July 5 against the Kursk salient and constituted the final attempt by the German Army to recover the operational initiative on the Eastern Front. But before turning our attention to this, it is desirable to examine briefly the events that occurred during the first three months of 1943 along the somewhat circuitous front line running from north of Kursk to Lake Ladoga. These were deliberately omitted from Chapter 83 so as to give full effect to the account of the Battle of Stalingrad and its consequences.

On this front Army Groups "Centre" and "North", still commanded by Field-Marshals von Kluge and von Küchler respectively, were composed of seven armies (23 corps of 117 divisions or their equivalent on January 1, nine of them Panzer and eight motorised). The extremely winding course of the line on which the Germans had stabilised their positions at the end of March 1942 meant that it could not be held in any depth. To make matters worse, the lakes, rivers, and marshy tracts, so characteristic of the region, freeze hard and allow not only infantry and cavalry to pass over them but also lorries, artillery, and even tanks.

On January 4, the 3rd Panzerarmee on Kluge's left flank was broken through by troops of the 3rd Shock Army (Kalinin Front) on either side of Velikiye-Luki. A fortnight later, after every attempt to relieve the citadel of the town had failed, its defenders, reduced to 102 in number, managed to find their way back to the German lines, leaving 200 wounded behind them.

Of graver consequence was the defeat inflicted on the German 18th Army (Colonel-General G. Lindemann) to the south of Lake Ladoga. At O.K.H. this sector was known as the "bottleneck" on account of the pronounced salient formed by the front between Mga and the southern shore of the lake. But to evacuate it would have meant abandoning the siege of Leningrad; and for this reason Hitler had always opposed any suggestion that it should be done. XVI Corps (General Wodrig) held the salient and was hence liable to be cut off as soon as the Neva, which covered its left flank, no longer constituted an obstacle to the enemy.

Voroshilov relieves Leningrad

The task of co-ordinating the combined action of the Leningrad Front (Lieutenant-General M. A. Govorov) and the Volkhov Front (General K. A. Meretskov) was entrusted to Marshal K. Voroshilov. Govorov's 67th Army (Lieutenant-General V. P. Sviridov) was ordered to make contact with the 2nd Shock Army (Lieutenant-General I. I. Fedyuninsky) and the 8th Army (Lieutenant-General F. N. Starikov) both under the command of General Meretskov. According to a chart drawn up in Moscow, the operation involved 12 divisions and one infantry brigade taking on four German divisions. And whereas the Soviet divisions in all probability numbered some 10,000 men each, those of the Reich were severely reduced. In particular, the Russians could deploy almost 100 guns and mortars per mile, and each of the two fronts had its own air cover and support.

Hence the Russian attack on January 12, 1943 was backed by massive firepower and followed a sustained artillery bombardment lasting 90 minutes. Nevertheless, XVI Corps held the attack, with Lindemann, then Küchler, soon coming to its aid. Consequently it took a full week for the 2nd Shock Army advancing from the west and the 67th Army from the east to fight their way across the ten miles that divided them. On January 17, General Sviridov's troops entered Petrokrepost'; the following day, the entire population of Leningrad, delirious with joy, learnt that after 17 months' trials and privations borne with fortitude and stoicism, the siege had been broken. On February 6, railway communications between Peter the Great's capital city and the outside world were re-established. But the Russians were halted short of Mga, which meant that Leningrad's lifeline was restricted to a corridor six to seven miles wide. Stalin, however, was so pleased with the result that 19,000 decorations were awarded to the victorious troops who had raised the siege of Russia's second city.

This disaster, in which the 41st and 277th Infantry Divisions were almost entirely destroyed, and still more the rapid and tragic succession of defeats suffered south of Kursk, induced Hitler to agree to certain adjustments to the front line which he had obstinately refused to allow his generals to make the previous year, on the grounds that enormous quantities of matériel might be lost in the course of withdrawal.

The orders go out for Operation "Zitadelle"

In any event, this agonising question did not preoccupy Hitler who, on April 15, put his signature to the 13 copies of Operational Order No. 16. The document is a long one, as are all those which Hitler wrote, and the following extract will serve to illuminate the events that subsequently took place:

"I am resolved, as soon as the weather allows, to launch Operation 'Zitadelle', as the first offensive action of this year," were his opening words. "Hence the importance of this offensive. It must lead to a rapid and decisive success. It must give us the initiative for the coming spring and summer. In view of this, preparations must be conducted with the utmost precaution and the utmost energy. At the main points of attack the finest units, the finest weapons, the finest commanders will be committed, and plentiful supplies of munitions will be ensured. Every commander, every fighting man must be imbued with the capital significance of this offensive. The victory of Kursk must be as a beacon to the whole world.

"To this effect, I order:

1. Objective of the offensive: by means of a highly concentrated, and savage attack vigorously conducted by two armies, one from the area of Belgorod, the other from south of Orel, to encircle the enemy forces situated in the region of Kursk and annihilate them by concentric attacks.

"In the course of this offensive a new and shorter front line will be established, permitting economies of means, along the line joining Nejega, Korocha, Skorodnoye, Tim, passing east of Shchigry, and Sosna."

Under Point 2, the Führer went on to define the conditions necessary for the success of the enterprise:

"(a) to ensure to the full the advantage of surprise, and principally to keep the enemy ignorant of the timing of attack;

(b) to concentrate to the utmost the attacking forces on narrow fronts so as to obtain an overwhelming local superiority in all arms (tanks, assault guns, artillery, and rocket launchers) grouped in a single echelon until junction between the two armies in the rear of the enemy is effected, thereby cutting him off from his rear areas;

(c) to bring up as fast as possible, from the rear, the forces necessary to cover the flanks of the offensive thrusts, thus enabling the attacking forces to concentrate solely on their advance;

(d) by driving into the pocket from all sides and with all possible speed, to give the enemy no respite, and to accelerate his destruction;

(e) to execute the attack at a speed so rapid that the enemy can neither prevent encirclement nor bring up reserves from his other fronts; and

(f) by the speedy establishment of the new front line, to allow the disengagement of forces, especially the Panzer forces, with all possible despatch, so that they can be used for other purposes."

Then the Führer fixed the parts to be played by Army Groups "Centre" and "South" and the Luftwaffe, apportioned the means at their disposal, and laid down certain requirements for misleading the enemy as to the German intentions, and for the maintenance of secrecy. As from April 28, Kluge and Manstein were to be ready to launch the attack within six days of receiving the order from O.K.H., the earliest date suggested for the offensive being May 3.

Manstein expresses his preferences

Manstein had during the previous February and March declared his preference for a plan of operations radically different to that outlined in the order of April 15. He had told Hitler of this on the occasion of the Führer's visit to his H.Q. in Zaporozh'ye. In substance, his idea was to await the offensive that the enemy was bound to launch in order to recover the Donets basin. Once this had got under way, the Germans would conduct an orderly retreat to the Melitopol'–Dniepropetrovsk line, while at the same time a powerful armoured force would be assembled in the Poltava–Khar'kov region. Once the Russians had been led into the trap, this force would counter-attack with lightning speed in the direction of the Sea of Azov, and the superiority which German commanders had always shown over their Russian counterparts in mobile warfare would bring them victory.

"The guiding principle of this operation was radically different from that of the German offensive in 1942. We would attack by a counter-stroke at the moment when the enemy had largely engaged and partially expended his assault forces. Our objective would no longer be the conquest of distant geographical points but the destruction of the Soviet southern wing by trapping it against the coast. To prevent his escape eastwards, as was the case in 1942, we would entice him to the lower Dniepr, as it would be impossible for him to resist this.

"If the operation succeeded, with the consequent heavy losses he would sustain, we could perhaps strike a second blow northwards, towards the centre of the front."

Certainly Manstein was under no illusion that the method he advocated could decide the war in favour of the Third Reich; but at least the situation would again be in Germany's favour and she would obtain what Manstein terms a "putting off" and Mellenthin a "stalemate", enabling her to bide her time. But Hitler did not agree with this line of argument, countering it with his usual economic arguments: Nikopol' manganese, for instance — "to lose Nikopol' would be to lose the war" was his last word, and at the meeting in Munich, Manstein did not raise his plan again.

Massive Russian defence lines

According to a perfectly correct comment in the Great Patriotic War, when spring came round again, Stalin had more than sufficient means at hand to take the initiative. But confronted by the German preparations against the Kursk salient

Russian forces 'Guardsmen' attack.

reported to him by General N. F. Vatutin, new commander of the Voronezh Front, from April 21 onwards Stalin felt, the same work assures us, that it "was more expedient to oppose the enemy with a defensive system constructed in due time, echeloned in depth, and insuperable. On the basis of propositions made to it by the commanders at the front, Supreme Headquarters resolved to wear the enemy out decisively in the course of his assault, by defensive action, then to smash him by means of a counter-offensive."

Hence, by a curious coincidence, Stalin came round to the idea of "return attack" at the very time that Hitler refused to let Manstein attempt to apply it. With the Panzers smashed in the salient around Kursk, it would be a far easier task to defeat Army

Groups "Centre" and "South" and attain the objectives that had been set for the end of autumn 1943: Smolensk, the Sozh, the middle and lower Dniepr, and Kerch' Strait, thus liberating the eastern parts of White Russia and the Ukraine, the Donets basin, and what the Germans still held in the Kuban'.

It is true that in adopting these tactics, Stalin had the advantage of detailed information as to the strength and intentions of the adversary and that he followed the "Zitadelle" preparations very closely: "Rössler," write Accoce and Quiet, "gave them full and detailed description in his despatches. Once again, Werther, his little team inside O.K.W., had achieved a miracle. Nothing was missing. The sectors to be attacked, the men and matériel to be used, the position of the supply columns, the chain of command, the positions of reinforcements, D-day, and zero hour. There was nothing more to be desired and the Russians desired nothing more. They simply waited, confident of victory."

And their confidence was all the greater because first-hand information and reports from partisans confirmed the radio messages of their conscientious informer in Lucerne. Accoce and Quiet make no exaggeration. From a memo of the period it appears that in July 1943 Stalin believed he had 210 enemy divisions, excluding Finns, facing him. The official O.K.W. record for July 7 of that year gives 210 exactly, plus five regiments.

Hitler's delays allowed the Russians to organise the battlefield on which the attack was anticipated and to do so to a depth of between 16 and 25 miles. A cunning combination of minefields was intended to channel the German armoured units onto what the Russians called "anti- tank fronts", solid defence sectors particularly well provided with anti-tank guns.

The defence of the Kursk salient, which had a front of about 340 miles, was entrusted to the Central and Voronezh Fronts. The Central Front, under the command of General Rokossovsky, had five armies deployed forward, a tank army in second echelon, and two tank corps and a cavalry corps in reserve. The Voronezh Front (General Vatutin) had four armies forward, two more armies (one of them a tank army) in second echelon, and two tank and one rifle corps in reserve. The Steppe Front (Colonel-General I. S. Konev), positioned east of Kursk, constituted the Stavka reserve, and comprised five (including one tank) armies, plus one tank, one mechanised, and three cavalry corps in reserve.

Air support was provided by some 2,500 planes from the 2nd and 16th Air Armies. Even now, Soviet historians, who are so precise in the case of the German Army, decline to tell us the number of divisions and tanks involved in this battle; nevertheless, if we take a figure of roughly 75 infantry divisions and 3,600 tanks, this would appear to be about right. The Great Patriotic War, however, drops its reserve in speaking of the artillery. If we believe what we read, and there is no reason not to do so, Rokossovsky and Vatutin could count on no fewer than 20,000 guns, howitzers, and mortars, including 6,000 anti-tank guns, and 920 rocket launchers. For example, in order to bar the axis along which it was expected that Model's main thrust would be developed, Rokossovsky allocated to Pukhov's 13th Army a whole additional corps of artillery, totalling some 700 guns and mortars. The defensive potential of the Red Army thus surpassed the offensive potential of the Germans, and their complete knowledge of Field-Marshals von Kluge's and von Manstein's dispositions and proposed axes of advance enabled the Russians to concentrate their artillery and armoured units so as to prevent them moving in the direction intended. In the evening of July 4 a pioneer from a Sudeten division deserted to the Russians and revealed the zero hour for Operation "Zitadelle ".

Failure all the way

Now that most of the pieces on the chessboard are in place we can deal quickly with the actual sequence of events in the Battle of Kursk which, on July 12, ended in an irreversible defeat for the Wehrmacht. Far from taking the enemy by surprise, the German 9th Army, following close on the desertion mentioned above, was itself surprised by a massive artillery counter-barrage, which struck its jump-off points in the final stages of preparation 20 minutes before zero hour. By evening, XLVII and XLI Panzer Corps, consisting of seven armoured divisions, had advanced only six miles across the defences of the Soviet 13th Army, and their 90 "Ferdinands" or "Elefants", being without machine guns, were unable to cope with the Russian infantry. More important, XXIII Corps, guarding the left flank, was stopped short of Malo-Arkhangelsk. On July 7, spurred on by the vigorous leadership of General Rauss, XLVII Panzer Corps reached the outskirts of Olkhovatka, less than 12 miles from its start line. There the German 9th Army was finally halted.

Army Group "South's" part of "Zitadelle" got off to a better start, thanks largely to impeccable co-ordination between tanks and dive-bombers. In the course of engagements which Manstein in his memoirs describes as extremely tough, Gruppe Kempf succeeded in breaking through two defence lines and reaching a point where it could intercept Steppe Front reinforcements coming to the aid of Voronezh Front. On July 11 the situation might be thought to be promising.

For 48 hours the 4th Panzerarmee met a solid wall of resistance of which General F. W. von Mellenthin, at that time chief-of-staff to XLVIII Panzer Corps, provides the following description in his book Panzer Battles:

"During the second and third days of the offensive we met with our first reverses. In spite of our soldiers' courage and determination, we were unable to find a gap in the enemy's second

Russian troops take cover under a tank.

defence line. The Panzergrenadier Division "Grossdeutschland" (Lieutenant-General Hoerlein) which had gone into battle in extremely tight formation and had come up against an extremely marshy tract of ground, was stopped by prepared fortifications defended with anti-tank guns, flame-throwers, and T-34 tanks, and was met by violent artillery fire. For some time it remained unable to move in the middle of the battlefield devised by the enemy. It was no easy task for our pioneers to find and fix a passable route through numerous minefields or across the tracts of marshland. A large number of tanks were blown up by mines or destroyed by aerial attacks: the Red Air Force showed little regard for the fact of the Luftwaffe's superiority and fought the battle with remarkable determination and spirit."

On July 7, however, XLVIII Panzer Corps and on its right II Waffen S.S. Panzer Corps found themselves unopposed, after repulsing heavy counterattacks by tanks which developed as pincer movements. Thus on July 11, after establishing a bridgehead on the Psel and getting close to Oboyan, the 4th Panzerarmee had advanced 18 to 20 miles through Vatutin's lines, while Gruppe Kempf, without having been able to land on the western bank of the Korocha had nevertheless managed to fulfil its primary task of protecting the 4th Panzerarmee's right flank. Two days later, Manstein reported that since D-day he had taken 24,000 prisoners and destroyed or captured 100 tanks and 108 anti-tank guns, and intended to move up his reserve, XXIV Panzer Corps.

These, however, were limited successes and "Zitadelle" was a serious reverse for Hitler. Between the spearhead of the 4th Panzerarmee, on the edge of Oboyan, and the vanguard of the 9th

Army, forced to halt before Olkhovatka, the gap between the two armies remained, and would remain, 75 miles.

Far from feeling discouragement, Vatutin made known to Stavka in the evening of July 10 his intention of counterattacking, and bringing up for this purpose his 5th Guards Tank Army (Lieutenant-General P. A. Rotmistrov) with its 850 tanks and assault guns, as well as the 1st Tank Army (Lieutenant-General M. E. Katukov).

On the other side of the battlefield, Rokossovsky addressed the following rousing order of the day to his troops on July 12: "The soldiers of the Central Front who met the enemy with a rampart of murderous steel and truly Russian grit and tenacity have exhausted him after a week of unrelenting and unremitting fighting; they have contained the enemy's drive. The first phase of the battle is over."

And indeed, on that same July 12, the Soviet armies of the Bryansk and West Front, following a predetermined plan, proceeded to launch a major offensive against the German-held Orel salient.

The end of the greatest tank battle

Thus ended the Battle of Kursk which, involving as it did more than 5,400 armoured and tracked vehicles, must be counted the greatest tank battle of World War II.

Some commentators have compared it with the ill-starred offensive launched by General Nivelle which ground to a halt on April 16, 1917 on the steep slopes up to the Chemin des Dames. But it would seem to bear greater similarity to Ludendorff's final attempt to give victory to the German Army. On July 15, 1918, the Quartermaster-General of the Imperial German Army was brought to a standstill in Champagne by Pétain's system of defence in depth, and this failure allowed Foch to detach Mangin and Degoutte in a French offensive against the Château-Thierry salient. Subsequently the new Marshal of France extended his battle-line to left and to right, and the German retreat lasted until the Armistice on November 11, 1918.

There is one difference between these two sets of circumstances. On August 10, 1918, on receiving the news that Sir Douglas Haig's tanks had scattered the German defence in Picardy, Wilhelm II declared to Hindenburg and to Ludendorff: "This to my mind is the final reckoning", and this flash of common sense spared Germany the horrors of invasion. In July 1943, Hitler, the head of state, was incapable of making a similar observation to Hitler, the war leader, still less of parting company with him as the Kaiser parted company with Ludendorff on October 26, 1918.

The Panzer defeat in the Kursk salient has had its historians in both camps, but it also had its prophet, who in the spring of 1939 mused on the question of what might be the result should an army of tanks collide with a similar army given a defensive function. And in the course of examining this hypothesis which he declared had been neglected, he arrived at the following conclusion and another question: "On land, there does exist a means of halting a tank offensive: a combination of mines and anti-tank guns. What would happen to an offensive by tank divisions which encountered a defence composed of similar tank divisions, but ones which had been carefully deployed and had had time to work out a considered fire-plan on the chosen battlefield, on which anti-tank firepower was closely co-ordinated with natural obstacles reinforced by minefields?"

Thus, three or four months before the war broke out, Marshal Pétain expressed himself in a preface to General Chauvineau's book Is an Invasion Still Possible? that is often quoted and never read. And the event itself would prove him right-but on a scale beyond the wildest imaginings in 1939: to stop 1,800 German tanks it required 3,600 Soviet tanks, 6,000 anti-tank weapons, and 400,000 mines!

Russian troops prepare artillery piece for firing.

The first five months of 1944 were marked by new Red Army offensives to the south of the Pripet Marshes. The offensives led to the liberation of the Ukraine and Crimea as well as to the conquest of the northern part of Rumanian Moldavia, while in the Leningrad region they succeeded in throwing the Germans back from a line linking Oranienbaum–Volkhov–Novgorod–Lake Ilmen onto one linking Narva–Lake Peipus and Pskov. At the same time, the Western Allies were also putting the pressure on Germany.

Further south, General Sir Henry Maitland Wilson, new Allied Commander-in-Chief in the Mediterranean, endeavoured to carry out the limited mission which had been entrusted to him in implementation of decisions recently taken at the Teheran Conference. Two days before the Normandy landings, the advance guard of his 15th Army Group under General Sir Harold Alexander had entered Rome hard on the enemy's heels. Thereby the allies had achieved their strictly geographical objective, but arguably at the price of sacrificing their strategic objective in Italy, namely the destruction of the enemy forces.

Parallel to this, in Great Britain the preparations for Operation "Overlord", with all their attendant difficulties, were rapidly approaching their climax. While the divisions taking part in the landings by sea and by air were undergoing intensive training, in London Generals Eisenhower and Montgomery were putting the final touches to the invasion plans drawn up by the American and British Combined Chiefs-of-Staff, C.O.S.S.A.C., and submitted for their approval by General Morgan.

Bombing stepped up

Anglo-American bomber formations intensified their missions by day and by night over the Third Reich as well as over occupied Europe. Most probably the results obtained over the first six months were no more significant in their impact on German war production than during the previous year. However, systematic pinpointing of synthetic oil plants from spring onwards, as well as of the Ploieti oil-wells, enabled the Allied air forces for the first time to influence events on land directly by precipitating an extremely serious fuel crisis in the Wehrmacht. Furthermore, in the western and southern theatres British and American fighter-bombers and medium bombers constantly pounded the enemy's communications system. In France and Belgium their aim was to obstruct rapid reinforcement of the German 7th Army, which was in position on the coast between Cabourg and St. Nazaire; in Italy their main targets were the Po bridges and the course of the Adige, the route by which enemy supplies and reinforcements moved after crossing the Brenner Pass. Moreover, the Luftwaffe was being forced to sacrifice itself against the mass American daylight raids escorted by long-range fighters.

Katyn: the Burden of Guilt

On April 13, 1943 the Germans found piled up 12 deep the mummified bodies of 4,143 Polish officers, all felled by pistol shots to the back of the neck. It was later revealed that they had been murdered by the Soviet N.K.V.D.

The Führer and Russia

But when it came down to it, the Russians' third winter offensive, the Führer showed the same persistent and mistaken obstinacy as he had done in the previous years, bringing his familiar arguments of high politics and the war economy to bear against his army group commanders every time one of them sought to advise him of a suitable chance to disengage in the face of the sheer weight, regardless of cost, of the Soviet onslaught.

And evidence of this came with the fresh disasters that occurred, principally to the south of the Pripet Marshes, when towards the end of January 1944 Kanev and Korsun' and, on the following May 13, Sevastopol' found their doleful place in the annals of German military history. So it was again a case of immediately arresting the possible consequences of these new defeats sustained by the Third Reich and, since the few reinforcements still available on the Eastern Front were quite inadequate, Hitler the head of O.K.H. sought help from Hitler the head of O.K.W. in order to avert imminent catastrophe. In these circumstances, born of his quite inexcusable obstinacy, Hitler the supreme commander had no alternative but to depart from the principle he had laid down in his Directive of November 3,1943. At the end of the winter of 1943, the Waffen-S.S. II Panzer Corps had to be transferred from the Alençon sector, and hence missed the rendezvous of June 6, 1944 in Normandy.

Manstein's impossible task

The Soviet winter offensive began on December 24, 1943 on either side of the Kiev-Zhitomir road and within a few weeks

German self-propelled gun Sturmgeschutz in action in counterattack, Vitebsk area.

involved the whole of Army Group "South" which, at that time, stretching as it did between the estuary of the Dniepr and the Mozyr' region, comprised the 6th Army (General Hollidt), the 1st Panzerarmee (General Hube), the 8th Army (General W6hler), and the 4th Panzerarmee (General Raus). The entire group, commanded as before by Field-Marshal Erich von Manstein, was made up of 73 of the 180 understrength divisions that were then engaged on the front between Kerch' Strait and the Oranienbaum bridgehead on the Baltic.

In particular, 22 of the 32 Panzer and Panzergrenadier divisions on the Eastern Front were allocated to Army Group

"South".

The 18th Artillery Division had also been assigned there, with its eight tracked or motorised battalions, comprising nine 21-cm howitzers, plus 3015-cm, 4810.5-cm, and 12 10-cm guns. This was a new formation, based on similar ones in the Red Army, and much was expected of it. But it proved disappointing and was disbanded after a few months. A total of 73 divisions seems impressive, but the figure is misleading. Between July 31, 1943 and July 31, 1944, Manstein lost 405,409 killed, wounded, and missing, yet in the same period his reinforcements in officers, N.C.O.s, and other ranks amounted to only 221,893. His divisions, particularly the infantry ones, were thin on the ground. It was the same story with the Panzer divisions, which in spite of increased production of tanks, were 50 to 60 per cent below complement. And the front to be defended, in the Führer's words "with no thought of retreat", measured a good 650 miles.

4th Panzerarmee defeated

As has been noted, the 1st Ukrainian Front (General N. F. Vatutin) inaugurated the Soviet winter offensive on December 24. With fire support from four artillery divisions and ten artillery regiments (936 guns and howitzers) assigned from general reserve, Vatutin launched an attack on an 18-mile front in the direction of Zhitomir, with 18 divisions (38th Army and 1st Guards Army) backed by six armoured or mechanised corps. The XXIV Panzer Corps (General Nehring: 8th and 19th Panzer

Divisions and Waffen-S.S. 2nd Panzer Division "Das Reich') put up a stubborn resistance for 48 hours, then, in spite of

being reinforced by XLVIII Panzer Corps (General Balck) broke under the impact. The 3rd Guards Tank Army (General Rybalko) stormed through the breach and on the last day of the year recaptured Zhitomir and by January 3 reached Novograd-Volinskiy, over 85 miles from its jumping-off point. Further to the right, the Soviet 60th and 13th Armies, comprising 14 infantry divisions, had retaken Korosten and were close to the Russo-Polish frontier of the pre-war period. On Rybalko's left, Vatutin's centre was overwhelming the defenders of Berdichev.

Hence the defeat of the 4th Panzerarmee took on a strategic dimension, and in the event of Vatutin exploiting his success to the south-west resolutely and with vigour, could have led to the total destruction of Army Groups "South" and "A". As early as December 25, Manstein had been aware of the possibility of such a danger and had alerted O.K.H. to this effect, confronting it with the following dilemma: "The 4th Army was no longer capable of defending the flank of Army Groups 'South' and 'A'; effective reinforcements were vital. If O.K.H. was unable to provide these, we would be obliged to take five or six divisions at least from our right wing, which clearly could not then maintain its positions inside the Dniepr loop. We sought our liberty of movement for that wing."

Manstein a defeatist?

In Manstein's dispute with Hitler, are there grounds for accusing the former — as has been alleged from time to time — of having been obsessed with withdrawal in the face of any build-up in enemy strength or else of having been unjustifiably alarmed by the spectre of encirclement?

It is clear that at this juncture Manstein no longer displayed the genius for bold moves that had characterised his performance between 1941 and 1943; yet it is also abundantly clear that he was no longer in a position where he could act boldly. Apart from XLVI Panzer Corps, which had recently been assigned to him, he knew that he could expect no further reinforcements from the west and that on the Eastern Front it was a case of robbing Peter to pay Paul. The liquidation of a pocket containing half a dozen divisions would mean not only the loss of some 60,000 men and most of their matériel, but, further, a breach of 75 to 90 miles in his now dangerously reduced defensive system. The battle of Korsun'–Shevchenkovskiy would show that his appreciation of the situation-and he had vainly tried to prevail on Hitler to accept it-was the correct one.

On January 25, Marshal Zhukov, who had been delegated by Stavka to co-ordinate operations, threw the troops of the 1st and 2nd Ukrainian Fronts into an assault on the Kanev salient. General Vatutin brought his 40th Army (Lieutenant-General E. F. Zhmachenko) and 27th Army (Lieutenant-General S. G. Trofimenko) to bear on the western front of the salient. They had a considerable job in overcoming German resistance so as to open a breach for brigades of the 6th Tank Army (Lieutenant-General A. G. Kravchenko) to move south-eastwards. The 2nd Ukrainian Front, under General Konev, seems to have had an easier task; delivering its attack at the point of junction of XLVII Panzer Corps and XI Corps, the 4th Guards Army (Major-General A. I. Ryzhov) and 53rd Army (Major-General I. V. Galanin) swiftly

Russian T34 tanks advance.t

broke through the lines held by the 389th Infantry Division, thus enabling the 5th Guards Tank Army, under the command of General P. A. Rotmistrov, to be unleashed without further ado.

"There could be no other adequate analogy. The sea-dikes had given and the tide, interminable and vast, spread across the plain, passing either side of our tanks which, with packets of infantry round them, had the appearance of reefs rising from the swell. Our amazement was at its peak when in the afternoon cavalry units, galloping westwards, broke through our screen of fire in close formation. It was a sight long-forgotten, almost a mirage — V Guards Cavalry Corps, with the 11th, 12th, and 63rd Cavalry Divisions under the command of Selimanov."

Hitler hangs on to Kanev

Hitler was determined to defend the Kanev salient at all costs, as he considered it the base for launching an offensive which would force the Russians to cross back over the Dniepr in the region of Kiev. Hence orders were given to Stemmermann to hold his positions and to establish himself so as to be able to repulse any attacks from the south; to General O. Wbhler, commanding the 8th Army, to hurl his XLVII Panzer Corps, reinforced to a strength of five Panzer divisions, at the eastern face of the pocket; and to General H. V. Hube, to drive his III Panzer Corps, comprising four Panzer divisions (among them the 1st S.S. Panzer Division "Leibstandarte Adolf Hitler") at the western face of the pocket.

Such a plan, involving the concentration of nine Panzer divisions against the Kanev pocket, was nevertheless doomed to failure within the time limit imposed by the defenders' capacity to hold out, though an airlift was being organised to keep them in supplies. Moreover, most of the Panzer divisions designated by Hitler were already engaged elsewhere, and hence it was a case of relieving them, pulling them out of line, and moving them to their jump-off points. Furthermore, they were far short of complement; in particular their grenadier regiments were reduced to only several hundred rifles, and there were grounds for feeling some apprehension that they lacked the resilience necessary for a rapid thrust. Yet in counter-attacks speed is all.

Indeed, on February 2, XLVII and III Panzer Corps still had only four Panzer divisions and, what is more, one of them was immediately withdrawn from General N. von Vormann's XLVII

Russain advances past German tank.

Thus, in a monograph dealing with this episode, the former commander of XLVII Panzer Corps describes the breakthrough at Krasnosilka (30 miles north-west of Kirovograd). In these conditions, it is not surprising that Vatutin's and Konev's tanks effected a meeting on January 28 in the region of Zvenigorodka. XI Corps, which formed the left of the German 8th Army, and XLII Corps, on the right of the 1st Panzerarmee, were caught in the trap along with four infantry divisions (the 57th, 72nd, 88th, and 389th), the 5th S.S. Panzergrenadier Division "Wiking" and the S.S. Fretwilligen Sturmbrigade "Wallonie", which Himmler had recruited in the French-speaking provinces of Belgium.

Panzer Corps by special order of the Führer, on receipt of the news that units of the 3rd Ukrainian Front were advancing on Apostolovo, which lies half-way between Nikopol' and Krivoy-Rog. The following night, the rasputitsa arrived, covering the western Ukraine with the sea of mud described above. Now the unseasonable weather worked to the advantage of the Russians, delaying their enemy's movements still further. When the earth grew hard again, around February 10, the Soviet encirclement of the Korsun' pocket was consolidated to such an extent that III Panzer Corps only managed to reach the area of Lysyanka, eight miles from the lines held by the besieged forces. p Not all the Russians welcomed the Red Army as liberators, and many, particularly from the western regions, fell back with the retreating Germans.

Break-out attempt

General Stemmermann, as one might expect, had not succeeded in forming a front to the south as he had been enjoined to do in his orders from Rastenburg, without at the same time abandoning Kanev and the banks of the Dniepr, which would have been in defiance of these orders. On February 8 he gave no reply to a summons to capitulate transmitted to him from General Konev, under orders to reduce the pocket. Both Stemmermann and his subordinates turned a deaf ear to the exhortations made to them by representatives of the "Committee for a Free Germany" who had been conveyed to the battlefield on Moscow's orders and were led by General von Seydlitz-Kurzbach, former commander of LI Corps, who had been taken prisoner at Stalingrad. The tracts

and individual free passes scattered among the soldiers with a view to encouraging surrender were equally ignored.

Notwithstanding, the airlift worked poorly in the face of an abundant and highly effective Soviet fighter force, and those encircled at Korsun' saw their strength diminish further each day. It was inevitable that the order should come to attempt to break out towards III Panzer Corps, which had been conclusively halted by the mud. It was the only chance left.

To this effect, General Stemmermann reassembled the remnants of his two corps round the village of Shanderovka and organised them in three echelons: at the head the grenadiers, bayonets fixed, next the heavy infantry units, and then finally the artillery and service troops. The 57th and 88th Infantry Divisions protected the rear and showed themselves equal to the sacrifice they were called upon to give. The attempt took place on the night of February 16–17, but at first light Soviet artillery, tanks, and aircraft were able to react with vigour and immediate effect:

"Till now," writes General von Vormann, "our forces had dragged all their heavy equipment across gullies filled with thick, impacted snow. But then enemy shelling proved our undoing. Artillery and assault guns were abandoned after they had exhausted their ammunition. And then the wounded moving with the troops met their fate … Veritable hordes of hundreds of soldiers from every type of unit headed westwards under the nearest available officer. The enemy infantry were swept out of the way by our advancing bayonets; even the tanks turned in their tracks. But all the same Russian fire struck with impunity at the masses, moving forward with heads down, unevenly and unprotected. Our losses multiplied …"

This hopeless charge by 40,000 men foundered on the natural obstacle of the Gniloy-Tikich, a stream which had thawed only a few days previously, and was now 25 feet wide and just deep enough for a man to drown in. And it heralded a fresh disaster, which the Belgian Léon Degrelle, fighting in the ranks of the S.S. Sturmbrigade "Wallonie", describes in unforgettable terms:

"The artillery teams which had escaped destruction plunged first into the waves and ice floes. The banks of the river were steep, the horses turned back and were drowned. Men then threw themselves in to cross the river by swimming. But hardly had they got to the other side than they were transformed into blocks of ice, and their clothes frozen to their bodies. They tried to throw their equipment over the river. But often their uniforms fell into the current. Soon hundreds of soldiers, completely naked and red as lobsters, were thronging the other bank. Many soldiers did not know how to swim. Maddened by the approach of the Russian armour which was coming down the slope and firing at them, they threw themselves pell-mell into the icy water. Some escaped death by clinging to trees which had been hastily felled … but hundreds were drowned. Under the fire of tanks thousands upon thousands of soldiers, half clothed, streaming with icy water or naked as the day they were born, ran through the snow towards the distant cottages of Lysyanka."

The hecatomb of Lysyanka

In short, between February 16 and 18, III Panzer Corps at Lysyanka retrieved only 30,000 survivors, unarmed for the most part; among them, General Lieb, commander of XLII Corps. The valiant Stemmermann had been killed by a piece of shrapnel. According to the Soviet historian B. S. Telpukhovsky, of the Moscow Academy of Sciences, on this one occasion the Russians accounted for more than 52,000 dead and 11,000 prisoners but his German colleagues Hillgruber and Jacobsen take issue with him: "Just before the investment occurred the two German corps numbered 54,000 all told, including rear area troops, some of whom escaped encirclement."

Allowing for the 30,000 or 32,000 survivors of this 21-day tragedy, German losses in the sector could barely have risen to more than one third of the total claimed by Moscow nearly 15 years after Germany's unconditional surrender. Hillgruber's and Jacobsen's figures are beyond question.

Alexander Werth quotes the account of a Soviet eye witness of these tragic events which confirms General von Vormann's account. On the day following, Major Kampov told Werth:

"I remember that last fateful night of the 17th of February. A terrible blizzard was blowing. Konev himself was travelling in a tank through the shell-shattered 'corridor'. I rode on horseback from one point in the corridor to another, with a dispatch from the General; it was so dark that I could not see the horse's ears. I mention this darkness and this blizzard because they are an important factor in what happened …

"It was during that night, or the evening before, that the encircled Germans, having abandoned all hope of ever being rescued by Hube, decided to make a last desperate effort to break out …

"Driven out of their warm huts they had to abandon Shanderovka. They flocked into the ravines near the village, and then took the desperate decision to break through early in the morning … So that morning they formed themselves into two marching columns of about 14,000 each …

"It was about six o'clock in the morning. Our tanks and our cavalry suddenly appeared and rushed straight into the thick of the two columns. What happened then is hard to describe. The Germans ran'in all directions. And for the next four hours our tanks raced up and down the plain crushing them by the hundred. Our cavalry, competing with the tanks, chased them through the ravines where it was hard for the tanks to pursue them. Most of the time the tanks were not using their guns lest they hit their own cavalry. Hundreds and hundreds of cavalry were hacking at them with their sabres, and massacred the Fritzes as no one had ever been massacred by cavalry before. There was no time to take prisoners. It was the kind of carnage that nothing could stop till it was all over. In a small area over 20,000 Germans were killed."

In connection with this episode, General von Vormann, in the study mentioned above, raises an interesting question. Observing that the encirclement of XI and XLII Corps on January 28 had opened a 65-mile breach between the right of III Panzer Corps and the left of XLVII, he considers why the Soviet high command failed to exploit the opportunity of a breakthrough afforded. In his opinion, on that day there was nothing to prevent Stalin driving his armoured units towards Uman' and across the Bug, assigning to them distant objectives on the Dniestr, the Prut, and in the Rumanian Carpathians. This not impossible objective would have sealed the fate of Army Groups "A" and "South".

This question was raised in 1954, but it is still impossible to provide an answer which documents can verify. We must be content with the supposition that Stalin acted with extreme prudence, by annihilating the Korsun' pocket before embarking on more hazardous enterprises, and it should be noted that 12 months from then Chernyakhovsky, Rokossovsky, Zhukov, and Konev had far more freedom of action. But by then, from Tilsit to the Polish Carpathians, the German Army was little more than a ruin.

What is certain is that Stalin showed himself eminently satisfied by the way in which Zhukov and those under him had conducted the business; the proof of it being that on February 23, 1944 a decree of the Praesidium of the Supreme Council of the U.S.S.R. conferred upon General of the Army Konev the title of Marshal of the Soviet Union and upon General Rotmistrov that of Marshal of Tank Forces. Even if the generals had missed a golden opportunity, they had certainly won a great victory.

Russian troops engaged in combat.

First offensive: Finland

The first blows of the Soviet summer offensive fell on Finland. As we have seen, thanks to the Swedish Government's action as an intermediary, negotiations were on the point of being concluded between Helsinki and Moscow in the late winter, and the Finns were no longer insisting on the return to the status quo of March 1940. The talks fell through, however, because Moscow demanded from this small unhappy country an indemnity of 600 million dollars' worth of raw materials and goods, spread over the next five years.

When spring came, the situation of Finland and her valiant army could hardly give rise to optimism. The defeat of Field-Marshal von Küchler and the German Army Group "North", driven from the banks of the Neva to those of the Narva, deprived Marshal Mannerheim of any hope of German help in the event of a Soviet offensive.

Mannerheim had therefore divided the bulk of his forces in two: in the isthmus between the Gulf of Finland and Lake Ladoga he had put six divisions, including his 1st Armoured Division, and two brigades, all under III and IV Corps; on the front of the river Svir', which runs from Lake Onega to Lake Ladoga, he had nine divisions and three brigades. This was a lot, to be sure but, Mannerheim Wrote:

"A reduction of the troops in East Karelia would, however, constitute a surrender of this strategically valuable area and be a good bargaining-point for the attainment of peace. The disposition of the troops was also based on the not unreasonable hope that the fortifications of the Isthmus would compensate for the weakness of man-power."

The Finnish III and IV Corps could in fact count on three successive lines of fortifications, the first two from 44 to 50 miles long and the third 75 miles. This was small stuff against the powerful forces massed by the Russians, especially in artillery, for the Leningrad Front, still under the command of General L. A. Govorov. Finnish Intelligence sources revealed that the Russians put some 20 infantry divisions on the Finnish front, together with four armoured brigades, five or six tank regiments, and four regiments of assault guns, that is some 450 armoured vehicles in all, and about 1,000 aircraft. For their part the official Soviet sources give no figures, so that we are inclined to believe the Finns. Silence implies consent.

Karelia overrun

On June 9 the Leningrad Front went over to the attack, with an artillery barrage of up to 250 guns per mile. Lieutenant-General D. N. Gussev and his 21st Army had been given the main task and this developed over a ten-mile front along the coastal sector, which allowed the Red Navy's Baltic Fleet to take part under the command of Admiral V. F. Tributs. Mannerheim wrote: "June 10th may with reason be described as the black day of our war history. The infantry assault, carried out by three divisions of the Guards against a single Finnish regiment, broke the defence and forced the front in the coastal sector back about six miles. Furious fighting raged at a number of holding lines, but the on-storming massed armour broke their resistance.

"Because of the enemy's rapid advance, the 10th Division

fighting on the coast sector lost most of its artillery. On June 11th, its cut-up units were withdrawn behind the V.T. (Vammelsuu-Taipale) position to be brought up to strength."

But hardly had the defenders of the isthmus taken up their positions than they were driven back by an attack which broke through north of the Leningrad–Viipuri (Vyborg) railway. The 1st Armoured Division counter-attacked, but to no avail. Faced with this rapidly deteriorating situation, Mannerheim left the defence of the isthmus to General Oesch and ordered the evacuation of Karelia. This enabled him to pull out four divisions. Before there could be any reployment in force in the threatened sector, the Russian 21st Army made a fresh breakthrough and seized Viipuri on June 20.

What would have happened to the defence if the armies of the Karelian Front (General K. A. Meretskov) had come into battle on the same day as the Leningrad Front and had trapped the Finnish V and VI Corps between Lakes Ladoga and Onega? For unknown reasons the Russians only started their attack five or six days after Mannerheim had ordered the defenders to break off contact.

The Russian offensive in eastern Karelia took the form of a pincer movement. One army crossed the Svir' and pushed northwards to meet the other which, having forced the Masselskaya defile, exploited this success southwards. But the pincers closed on a vacuum and at the beginning of July the Finns, though reduced to four divisions, had nevertheless succeeded in re-establishing their positions on a pre-arranged line from Lake Ladoga on their right to Lake Loymola on their left, some 45 miles from the present Soviet-Finnish frontier.

Field Marshall Mannerheim, Finnish president during World War II.

Between Lake Ladoga and the Gulf of Finland, Govorov had a few more successes, in particular establishing a bridgehead on the north bank of the Vuoksa, along which ran the third defensive position between Viipuri and Taipale. But finally everything quietened down and about July 15 General Oesch was able to state that the enemy forces opposite him were considerably thinner on the ground.

It would certainly be absurd to deny that the Red Army had won. The Finns had been driven back to their last line of defence and had lost the Karelia area, which they had intended to use as a counter in the forthcoming peace negotiations. The Soviet Union had also got the use of the Leningrad–Murmansk railway and canal which the Finns had begun in 1941.

In spite of the defeat, however, the fighting spirit of the Finnish Army lived on. It counter-attacked incessantly and in the whole campaign very few Finns were taken prisoners. On balance Moscow seems to have realised that to wipe out the Finnish Army would have cost more than the literal submission of Helsinki to the March 1940 conditions was worth.

Second offensive: Polotsk and the Pripet

On June 22,1944, as if to celebrate the third anniversary of the German aggression, Stalin opened his last great summer offensive between the Polotsk area and the north bank of the Pripet. This brought into action Bagramyan's 1st Baltic Front, Chernyakhovsky's 3rd Belorussian Front, Zakharov's 2nd Belorussian Front, and Rokossovsky's 1st Belorussian Front.

According to the Great Patriotic War, which we quote in Alexander Werth's version, the following were engaged in this offensive, including reserves: 166 infantry divisions, 31,000 guns and mortars, 5,200 tanks and self-propelled guns, and 6,000 aircraft. The Red Army had never before achieved such a concentration of force or had such huge quantities of supporting matériel, which included 25,000 two-ton lorries.

Michel Garder gives a lively account of the atmosphere of the Soviet summer offensive in his book A War Unlike The Others. He says:

"The patient work of the Red Army's general staff, which had prepared in great detail the grand plan of Stavka, resulted in this fantastic cavalcade. This was the true revenge for the summer of 1941! In the burning-hot July sky the Red Air Force was unopposed. White with dust the T-34's drove on westwards, breaking through the hedges, crushing down thickets, spitting out flame … with clusters of infantry clinging on to their rear platforms, adventure-bound. Swarms of men on motor-cycles … shouting cavalry … infantry in lorries … rocket-artillery cluttering up the road … the tracks … the paths … mowing down everything in their way.

"This was a long way from the stereotyped image of 'dejected troops herded to slaughter by Jewish political commissars'."

Marshal Vasilevsky had been sent to Bagramyan and Chernyakhovsky as Stavka's representative to co-ordinate their operations. Zhukov performed the same function with Zakharov and Rokossovsky.

The objective of the Soviet offensive was the destruction of Army Group "Centre", then commanded by Field-Marshal Busch, who in the early days of 1944 had taken over from Kluge at the latter's H.Q. at Minsk. Busch had four armies deployed from north to south as follows:

1. 3rd Panzerarmee (Colonel-General Reinhardt)
2. 4th Army (General von Tippelskirch)
3. 9th Army (General Jordan)
4. 2nd Army (Colonel-General Weiss)

By the end of the winter the withdrawals forced upon Army Groups "North" and "South" by the Soviet winter offensives had left Army Group "Centre" in a salient: the fortified area of Vitebsk on the Dvina was two-thirds encircled, whereas south of the Pripet Marshes Rokossovsky had got as far as the approaches to Kovel'. To counteract the threat to Field-Marshal Model's left at the end of March, Busch had been asked to send him eight divisions, including two Panzer. p The proof: German dead in the wake of the 2nd Belorussian Front's triumphant progress.

Russian superiority in tanks and aircraft

When the Soviet summer offensive started, Army Group "Centre" was thus reduced to 37 divisions. On June 22 the 2nd Army was not attacked, and so the initial clash in the battle for Belorussia was between 166 Soviet and 28 German divisions, on a front extending over 435 miles. The Russian divisions each had 10,000 men. Those of Generals Jordan, Tippelskirch, and Reinhardt were very much understrength, as can be seen in the account given by Major-General Heidkämper, chief-of-staff of the 3rd Panzerarmee. He showed that the Vitebsk salient was being held by LIII Corps along a front of 55 miles with the 206th, 4th and 6th Luftwaffe, and 246th Divisions, with 8,123 rifles

(about 150 rifles per mile). Reserves consisted of a battalion of heavy artillery, two heavy anti-tank companies, and one Luftwaffe special service battalion.

Colonel-General Reinhardt's VI and IX Corps were no better off, nor were the 4th and 9th Armies. German dispositions between the Pripet and the Dvina were thus as thin as a spider's web.

The mobile reserves which were to slow down then stop the onslaught of 4,500 Soviet tanks consisted of only the 20th Panzer and the 18th, 25th, and 60th Panzergrenadier Divisions with 400 tracked vehicles between them. For good measure add the same number of assault guns, and it will be seen that in armour the Germans were outnumbered by 5.6 to 1.

It was the same in the air: Luftflotte VI could get only an insignificant number of planes off the ground.

The offensive begins

During the night of June 19–20 the 240,000 partisans who controlled the forests in Belorussia cut the lines of communication of Army Group "Centre" in more than 10,000 places as far west as Minsk. At dawn on the 22nd the forces of the 1st Baltic and the 3rd Belorussian Fronts went over to the attack on both sides of Vitebsk. The 1st Belorussian Front went into action on the following day. Generals Bagramyan and Chernyakhovsky had been given as their first objective the capture of Vitebsk by a pincer movement, which would give their comrade Rokossovsky the time to pierce the German 9th Army's positions in the area of Bobruysk. When both these results had been achieved the two

Belorussian Fronts would let loose their armoured formations, which would converge in the direction of Minsk. A second pincer would thus be formed and this would crush Army Group "Centre". Bagramyan and Chernyakhovsky took just 48 hours to overpower the resistance of the 3rd Panzerarmee north-west and south-east of Vitebsk. During this brief spell the German commander also used up his meagre reserves as well as the 14th Division, sent to him by Busch as a reinforcement. Busch could ill afford the loss. In particular the German right wing, which consisted of VI Corps (General Pfeiffer, killed in this action), collapsed completely under the impact of the Soviet 5th Army and four armoured brigades, whose attack was preceded and supported by V Artillery Corps (520 heavy guns) and tactical air formations acting with a strength, a spirit, and an accuracy hitherto unknown on the Eastern Front.

Rokossovsky takes Bobruysk

Further south on the Belorussian front, the same causes could only produce the same effects and General Jordan, C.-in-C. 9th Army, was no luckier than Reinhardt; XXXV Corps, defending the fortified area of Bobruysk with four divisions, suffered the same fate as LIII Corps. When he opened his offensive on June 24, General Rokossovsky had taken good care not to launch his 1st Belorussian Front forces against the German fortified areas, but to push them into gaps north and south of the River Berezina. Three days of hard fighting brought him victory. South of Bobruysk he overcame XLI Panzer Corps (Lieutenant-General Hoffmeister) and cut off the retreating XXXV Corps (Lieutenant-

General von Lützow), leaving it trapped in the fortified area.

On June 29 16,000 Germans emerged from the pocket and gave themselves up, leaving behind them the bodies of 18,000 of their comrades. By now the mounted, motorised, mechanised, and armoured forces of General Pliev, one of the most brilliant cavalry commanders of the war, had reached Ossipovichi, some eight miles south-east of Minsk, and were rumbling forward to meet the 5th Guards Tank Army, which had passed Lepel' and was now in Borisov.

The situation of the German 4th Army, now at grips with greatly superior forces on the 2nd Belorussian Front, was scarcely any better. Faced with disasters on his right and left, General von Tippelskirch, now in command vice Colonel-General Heinrici, had to use all his initiative to get his army out of its positions along the River Proina and back to the Dniepr. The fortified areas of Mogilev and Orsha on the Dniepr, however, were soon overcome by Zakharov and Chernyakhovsky, and became the graveyards respectively of the 6th (Lieutenant-General Henie) and the 12th (Lieutenant-General Wagner) Divisions.

Tippelskirch thus had to continue his retreat westwards across rough forest land infested with marches and, particularly, thick with partisans. It is no wonder that, as planned by Stavka, Rotmistrov and Pliev got to Minsk before him on July 3, joining forces behind his back and condemning his XII and XXVII Corps and XXXIX Panzer Corps (respectively under Generals Vincenz Müller, Voelkers, Martinek) to the sad fate of "moving pockets".

A defeat worse than Stalingrad

It was June 28 before Hitler finally admitted that the Belorussian offensive was something more than a diversion. On that day he sacked General Busch, who had obeyed his directives unquestioningly, and replaced him by Field Marshal Model, who strove to limit the extent of the disaster. Army Group "North", though now uncovered on its right flank by the defeat of the 3rd Panzerarmee, was required to give up three divisions. Ten more, including four Panzer, were taken from Army Group "North Ukraine". These units were sent to the Belorussian front in the hope of an attack on the flank of Rokossovsky, who was now exploiting his victory along the line Minsk–Baranovichi–Brest–Litovsk. The breach now open between the Pripet and the Dvina was some 185 miles wide and, according to the O.K.H., this was swallowing up 126 infantry divisions and no fewer than 62 armoured or mechanised brigades with at least 2,500 tanks. On July 8 the last "moving pocket" surrendered behind the Russian lines with 17,000 men, having run out of ammunition. Out of 37 divisions in Army Group "Centre" on the previous June 22, 28 had been badly mauled, if not actually cut to pieces, and an enormous mass of matériel, including 215 tanks and more than 1,300 guns, had been captured.

According to statistics from Moscow, which appear reliable, the Germans lost between these two dates some 285,000 dead and prisoners, including 19 corps and divisional commanders. The Belorussian disaster was thus worse than Stalingrad and all the more so since, when Paulus resigned himself to the inevitable, the "Second Front" was still only a distant threat to the Third Reich.

Stalin celebrated in true Roman style by marching seemingly endless columns of 57,600 prisoners-of-war through the streets of Moscow with their generals at the head. Alexander Werth, the Sunday Times correspondent, was there and he described the behaviour of the Russian crowd as the men passed by:

"Youngsters booed and whistled, and even threw things at the Germans, only to be immediately restrained by the adults; men looked on grimly and in silence; but many women, especially elderly women, were full of commiseration (some even had tears in their eyes) as they looked at these bedraggled 'Fritzes'. I remember one old woman murmuring 'just like our poor boys … tozhe pognali ne voinu (also driven into war)'."

Red Army troops greeted by Belorussians.

Stalin gave Bagramyan, Chernyakhovsky, Zakharov, and Rokossovsky the job of exploiting as deeply and as fast as possible the victory at Minsk, the extent of which, thanks to Hitler, seems to have exceeded even Stavka's highest hopes.

Under the terms of the new directives, the forces of the 1st Baltic Front were given as their objective the Gulf of Riga, whilst the three Belorussian Fronts would move first on to the line Kaunas–Grodno–Brest-Litovsk, then force their way across the Niemen and the Bug, as they had done over the Dniepr and the Berezina. Colonel-General Chernyakhovsky would then take on the defences of eastern Prussia, whilst Zakharov and Rokossovsky (the latter just having been promoted Marshal of the U.S.S.R.) would invade Poland.

For three weeks the victors of Minsk covered their ten to fifteen miles a day, by-passing without much difficulty at first the units which Field-Marshal Model, like General Weygand after June 11, 1940, threw in piecemeal to stop the gaps. Model, the new C.-in-C. Army Group "Centre", now had the job of holding back the enemy long enough for O.K.H. to regroup its forces and to reform the indispensable continuous front. He was more highly regarded by Hitler than his unfortunate predecessor, and was thus able to obtain in time permission to evacuate a whole seri6s of so-called "fortified areas" which otherwise would have become so many death-traps for the army's divisions. This meant, of course, considerable sacrifices of territory:

July 13: Chernyakhovsky takes Vilnyus;

July 14: Rokossovsky envelops Pinsk, on the Pripet;

July 15: Chernyakhovsky forces the Niemen at Alytus, while Zakharovtakes Grodno;

July 18: Rokossovsky crosses the RussoPolish frontier fixed at Teheran;

July 23: Rokossovsky's advance guard enters Lublin;

July 27: Zakharov breaks through the defences of Bialystok;

July 28: Rokossovsky takes Brest-Litovsk;

July 31: Rokossovsky enters Praga, across the Vistula from Warsaw;

August 1: Chernyakhovsky reaches Kalvariya, 15 miles from the Prussian frontier; and

August 2: Chernyakhovsky takes Kaunas.

On Chernyakhovsky's right, General Bagramyan and the armies of the 1st Baltic Front poured through the breaches in the inner flanks of Army Groups "North" and "Centre" caused by the Vitebsk catastrophe. Whilst the means were lacking to stop the enemy's advance towards Riga, was it advisable to keep the German 16th and 18th Armies on the Polotsk–Pskov–Lake Peipus line, which they had been holding since their painful retreat of the preceding winter? Colonel-General Lindemann, C.-in-C. Army Group "North", concluded that it was not and advised the withdrawal of his forces on the left bank of the Dvina. He was also being asked to transfer certain of his units to Army Group "Centre", which strengthened his point of view.

But to abandon Estonia might risk the "defection" of Finland, as O.K.W. put it. And so on July 2 Hitler relieved Lindemann of his command and handed it over to General Friessner, who in February 1944 had distinguished himself as commander of Armeegruppe "Narva". This change of personnel did nothing to

Societ tank crews rest during advance.

improve the strategic situation.

On July 11 Bagramyan crossed the Dvina at Drissa and further to the left his advance guard reached Utena in Lithuania. On the following day the 2nd Baltic Front (General A. I. Eremenko) came into the battle and, breaking out from the area of Novosol'niki, drove deep into the positions of the German 16th Army (General Loch).

Caught up in front by Eremenko and behind by Bagramyan, the latter threatening his communications, Friessner, who had had to give up 12 divisions to Model, could only come to the same conclusions on July 12 as his predecessor had done. But, faced with the same refusal from Hitler to meet the situation with common sense, he did not hesitate, at the end of his letter dated that day, to stake his command:

"If, mein Führer," he wrote, "you are not prepared to accept my idea and give me the liberty of action necessary to carry out the measures proposed above, I shall be compelled to ask you to relieve me of the responsibilities I have assumed so far." Summoned by return of post to Rastenburg, Friessner upheld his view in the presence of the Führer, who reproached him for having used threats and for having shown an unmilitary attitude throughout. Reminding Hitler that he was responsible for some 700,000 men, and that he was fighting at the relative strength of one to eight, according to the account he has left of this interview he went so far as to say:

"I am not trying to hang on to my job. You can relieve me of it. You can even have me shot if you want to. But to ask me, in full knowledge of the facts and against the dictates of my conscience, to lead the men entrusted to me to certain destruction — that you can never do."

Hitler, with tears in his eyes, is thereupon supposed to have seized General Friessner's hand and promised him every support. But the facts are that each one stuck to his own position. And so Colonel-General Schörner, C.-in-C. Army Group "South Ukraine", was ordered on July 23 to change places immediately with Friessner, C.-in-C. Army Group "North", who was himself promoted to Colonel-General.

Konev attacks

On the German side of the immense front line stretching from the Baltic to the Carpathians, the second fortnight in July brought defeat to Army Group "North Ukraine". This added further disaster to the crushing of Army Group "Centre", the last consequences of which were still far from being played out. The tension was such that, taking also into account the American breakthrough in Normandy, it might have been thought that the last hour had struck for the Wehrmacht and for Greater Germany's Third Reich. This was how Marshal Rokossovsky saw events when he stated to a correspondent of the British Exchange Telegraph on July 26:

"It is no longer important to capture such and such a position. The essential thing is to give the enemy no respite. The Germans are running to their deaths … Their troops have lost all contact with their command."

On the following day a spokesman of Stavka spoke in the same terms at a press conference: "The Führer's G.H.Q. will no more be able to hold the line of the Vistula than it did those of the Bug and the San. The German Army is irremediably beaten and breaking up."

Also on July 13 Marshal Konev and the forces of the 1st Ukrainian Front had come into the battle, extending the action of the three Belorussian Fronts from the area of Kovel' to the left bank of the Dniestr. According to the Soviet military historian Boris S. Telpukhovsky, whose account we have no reason to doubt, Konev had been given by Stavka all the necessary men and matériel to secure an easy victory over Army Group "North Ukraine", which was still, together with Army Group "Centre", under the command of Model. For this assault Konev had 16,213 guns and rocket-launchers, 1,573 tanks, 463 assault guns, 3,240 aircraft, and no fewer than seven armies, including the 1st and 3rd Guards Tank Armies and the 4th Tank Army, commanded respectively by Generals M. E. Katukov, P. S. Rybalko, and D. D. Lelyushenko, all three very experienced tank commanders.

On the German side, Army Group "North Ukraine" had had to give up to Army Group "Centre" four Panzer and three infantry divisions since June 22 and was reduced to 43 divisions (of which five were Panzer and one Panzergrenadier) and two mountain brigades. Assuming that between April and June the German armoured divisions had been brought up to their normal strength of 160 fighting and command tanks which, knowing the aberrations of Adolf Hitler, seems highly unlikely, the Russians outnumbered them by two to one. In the air Russian superiority was of the order of five to one. Hence the disaster which befell 8th Panzer Division on July 14. Disregarding orders, it took the main road to Brody to speed up its counter-attack. Major-General von Mellenthin writes:

"Eighth Panzer was caught on the move by Russian aircraft and suffered devastating losses. Long columns of tanks and lorries went up in flames, and all hope of counterattack disappeared."

Marshal Konev had forces so powerful and so numerous at his command that he could give his offensive two centres of gravity. On the right, in the area southwest of Lutsk, a first group containing notably the 1st Guards Tank Army, was to break up the 4th Panzerarmee (General Harpe) then exploit its victory in a general south-west direction. On the left a second group, containing the 3rd Guards Tank Army and the 4th Tank Army, had concentrated in the area of Ternopol': attacking due west it was to engage the 1st Panzerarmee (Colonel-General Raus) and form a pincer with the first group.

The Russians reach the Vistula

Before these reinforcements could be put to use, Marshals Rokossovsky and Konev had reached the Vistula and the San at Blitzkrieg speed, mopping up German columns retreating on

Russian sappers - Checking for mines, booby traps.

foot or in horse-drawn vehicles. Between July 28 and 31, tanks of the 1st Belorussian Front covered the 120 miles between BrestLitovsk and the suburbs of Warsaw. They also crossed the Vistula at Magnuszew and Pulawy, upstream from the capital. Rokossovsky's optimistic view of events quoted above seems to have been justified. The 1st Ukrainian Front had similar quick successes, covering 125 miles on a front some 250 miles wide on July 27. On that same day its formations on the right got beyond Przemy l on the west bank of the San and cleaned up L'vov on the way, whilst on the left, having crossed the Dniestr, it captured Stanislawow and threw back to the Carpathians the Hungarian 1st and 2nd Armies, which had formed the right flank of Army Group "North Ukraine" since the end of the winter. The situation now looked very dangerous.

A few days later Konev got a bridgehead over 30 miles deep over the Vistula in the area of Sandomierz, drove on beyond the San as far as Rzeszów, more than 90 miles beyond L'vov, and on August 7 occupied the oil wells at Drogobycz and Boryslaw.

Warsaw — betrayed?

We are now brought to the controversy which arose between the West and the Soviets over the behaviour of Stalin, Stavka, and the Red Army towards the Warsaw rising started at 1700 hours on August 1 by General Bor-Komorowski, C.-in-C. of the Polish Home Army. We cannot imitate Telpukhovsky, who maintains a prudent silence on this subject but nevertheless devotes a page and a half of his extensive work to the liberation of the little Polish village of Guerasimowichy on July 26, 1944. In his memoirs,

Winston Churchill, reporting the return to Praga of Rokossovsky about September 15, made no bones about the reasons for the tragic episode as he saw them:

"The Russians occupied the Praga suburb, but went no further. They wished to have the non-Communist Poles destroyed to the full, but also to keep alive the idea that they were going to their rescue.

"Such was their liberation of Poland, where they now rule. But this cannot be the end of the story."

Churchill was doubtless writing under the influence of the exchange of telegraph messages he had had with Stalin on the subject of Warsaw, and was remembering the help he had wanted to give by air to the stricken city and its heroic defenders. He did not know then as well as we do now about the operations in the suburbs of the Polish capital between August 1 and 4. Michel Garder, writing in 1961 after carefully researching Soviet material published after 1953, agrees in broad essentials with Churchill. "With Rokossovsky within 32 miles of Warsaw," he writes, "it seemed to General Bor Komorowski that the arrival of the Russian troops could only be a matter of a few days. It was the duty of the Poles to welcome the Soviets as allies and not as 'liberator-occupiers'. This was just what Stalin did not want.

"In the eyes of the Kremlin, the Polish Home Army was merely a tool of the 'reactionary Polish clique' in London whose leaders, in addition to their 'enslavement to capitalism' and their 'bourgeois chauvinism' had had the effrontery to state that the Katyn massacres were the work of the N.K.V.D.

"Having suddenly run out of steam, the irresistible 1st

Belorussian Front offensive had found itself facing the German bridgehead in front of Warsaw. To get so far had, it is true, cost Rokossovsky's armies a great effort. Their lines of communication were stretched. They needed a few days' respite and probably considerable reinforcements in men and matériel to bring them back up to strength. But nothing, other than political considerations by the Kremlin, could justify the semi-inertia of the Soviet troops in September when they reached the suburbs of Praga."

Werth is less certain than Churchill or Garder. He seems to give credence to the pessimistic figures for the 1st Belorussian Front on August 1 quoted above from the Great Patriotic War.

On the other hand, he does not omit the passage which refers to the defeat of the Soviet 2nd Tank Army before Praga, where it was attacked on its left flank by five German divisions, including four Panzer. It is interesting to see that he was personally involved on one occasion. Received in Lublin by Rokossovsky he recorded the following on the spot:

"'I can't go into any details. But I'll tell you just this. After several weeks' heavy fighting in Belorussia and eastern Poland we finally reached the outskirts of Praga about the 1st of August. The Germans, at this point, threw in four armoured divisions, and we were driven back.'

'How far back?'

Soviet tanks march into Poland.

'I can't tell you exactly, but let's say nearly 100 kilometres (sixty-five miles).'

'Are you still retreating?'

'No-we are now advancing — but slowly.'

'Did you think on August 1 (as was suggested by the Pravda correspondent that day) that you could take Warsaw within a very few days?'

'If the Germans had not thrown in all that armour, we could have taken Warsaw, though not in a frontal attack; but it was never more than a 50–50 chance. A German counter-attack at Praga was not to be excluded, though we now know that before these armoured divisions arrived, the Germans inside Warsaw were in a panic, and were packing up in a great hurry.'

'Wasn't the Warsaw Rising justified in the circumstances?'

'No it was a bad mistake. The insurgents started it off their own bat, without consulting us.'

'There was a broadcast from Moscow calling on them to rise.'

'That was routine stuff (sic). There were similar calls to rise from Swit radio [Home Army], and also from the Polish service of the BBC — so I'm told, though I didn't hear it myself. Let's be serious. An armed insurrection in a place like Warsaw could only have succeeded if it had been carefully co-ordinated with the Red Army. The question of timing was of the utmost importance. The Warsaw insurgents were badly armed, and the rising would have made sense only if we were already on the point of entering Warsaw. That point had not been reached at any stage, and I'll admit that some Soviet correspondents were much too optimistic on the 1st of August. We were pushed back. We couldn't have

got Warsaw before the middle of August, even in the best of circumstances. But circumstances were not good, but bad. Such things do happen in war. It happened at Kharkov in March 1943 and at Zhitomir last winter.'

Whilst accepting the good faith and accuracy of Werth's report, it would seem that it should be interpreted as follows: Rokossovsky and, behind him, the Soviet high command, had well and truly got over their elation of July 26, and at a distance now of 30 days were claiming never to have felt it. However, at 2015 hours on July 15 Radio Moscow broadcast a stirring appeal to the population of Warsaw and a few hours later the Union of Polish Patriots station, which followed the Soviet line, took up the call:

"The Polish Army now entering Polish territory had been trained in the U.S.S.R. It unites with the People's Army to form the body of the Polish Armed Forces, the backbone of our nation in her struggle for independence. The sons of Warsaw will rally to its ranks tomorrow. Together with the allied army they will drive out the enemy to the west, expel Hitler's vermin from Poland and deal a mortal blow to the remains of Prussian imperialism. For Warsaw which did not yield, but fought on, the hour has struck."

And, as it was to be expected that the enemy, now cornered, would retreat into the capital, the appeal for an uprising continued: "This is why … by energetic hand-to-hand fighting in the streets of Warsaw, in the houses, the factories, the warehouses, not only shall we hasten the coming of our final liberation, but we shall safeguard our national heritage and the lives of our brothers."

Warsaw's epic fight

The rest is history. The defenders of Warsaw met their fate with the most sublime heroism. Having driven the Russians back over 30 miles from the right bank of the Vistula, the Germans calmly set about the reconquest of the Polish capital with large numbers of Tiger tanks, assault guns, and little Goliath tanks, a kind of remote-controlled bomb on tracks. The heaviest weapons the defenders had were of 20-mm calibre.

They fought from barricade to barricade, from house to house, from storey to storey and even in the sewers. The area occupied by the defenders gradually shrank, so that the meagre supplies dropped by Anglo-American aircraft fell increasingly into enemy hands. The repression of the uprising was entrusted to Himmler.

He appointed Waffen-S.S. General von dem Bach-Zalewski and gave him, amongst others, S.S. police units, a brigade of Russian ex-prisoners, and a brigade of ex-convicts, all of whom had committed such excesses that Guderian had persuaded Hitler to remove them from the front.

In the second fortnight of September the Russians reoccupied Praga but remained virtually passive opposite the capital. Under these conditions Bor-Komorowski, who had had 22,000 killed, missing, or seriously wounded out of his 40,000 fighters, resigned himself to surrender on October 2, obtaining from von dem Bach-Zalewski an assurance that his men would without exception be treated under the Geneva Convention of August 27. 1929 governing prisoners-of-war.

Warsaw uprising, Poland

THE BATTLE OF LAKE BALATON

By May 1945, the German resistance had collapsed before the Red Army. The ring was closing round the New Chancellery in Berlin, and Vienna, the second capital of the Nazi Greater Germany, had been under Marshal Tolbukhin's control since April 13.

Between the Drava and the Carpathians, General Wöhler, commanding Army Group "South", had tried to break the Budapest blockade during the first fortnight of January. Although he had been reinforced by IV S.S. Panzer Corps, which had been withdrawn from East Prussia just before the Soviet attack on the Vistula, he failed in this attempt. The German 6th Army, which had just been transferred to General Balck's command, nevertheless managed to regain possession of the important military position of Székesfehérvár, but the effort exhausted its strength.

This setback sealed the fate of IX S.S. Mountain Corps, which, under the command of General Pfeffer-Wildenbruch, made up the Hungarian capital's garrison. On February 13, Buda castle, the defenders' last stronghold, fell to Marshal Malinovsky's troops (2nd Ukrainian Front), whilst the 3rd Ukrainian Front under Marshal Tolbukhin cleared Pest. The Russians claimed the Germans had lost 41,000 killed and 110,000 prisoners. The figures are certainly exaggerated, but nevertheless the 13th Panzer Division, the "Feldherrnhalle" Panzergrenadier Division, and the 33rd Hungarian S.S. Cavalry Division had been wiped out.

On March 6, the 6th Panzerarmee (Colonel-General Sepp Dietrich) went over to the offensive from the bastion of Székesfehérvár. Dietrich had left the Ardennes front on about January 25; it had taken six weeks for him to travel and take up his position. He might, on the other hand have reached the Oder front between February 5 and 10 if the plan that Guderian had vainly recommended to the Führer had been followed. The Führer in fact expected a miracle from this new offensive, indeed even the recapture of the Ploie ti oilfields.

The 3rd Ukrainian Front was to be smashed under the impact of a triple attack:

1. the left, the 6th Panzerarmee, consisting of eight Panzer (including the "Leibstandarte Adolf Hitler", "Das Reich", "Hohenstaufen ", and "Hitlerjugend"), three infantry, and two cavalry divisions, was to deliver the main blow; it was to reach the Danube at Dunaföldvar and exploit its victory towards the south, with its left close to the Danube, its right on Lake Balaton;

2. between Lake Balaton and the Drava, the 2nd Panzerarmee (General de Angelis: six divisions) would immobilise Tolbukhin by attacking towards Kaposzvár; and

3. on the right, Army Group "E" (Colonel-General Löhr), in Yugoslavia, would send a corps of three divisions across the Drava, and from Mohacs move to the Danube.

The offensive of March 6 therefore committed 22 German divisions, including 19 from Army Group "South", out of the 39 that General Wöhler had under his command at the time. But this tremendous effort was of no avail. On the Drava and south of Lake Balaton, the German attack collapsed after 48 hours. The outlook for the 6th Panzerarmee seemed better on the day the engagement started, as the Panzers, massed on a narrow front, succeeded in breaking through, but the poorly-trained infantry proved incapable of exploiting this brief success. Tolbukhin, on the other hand, had organised his forces in depth and countered with his self-propelled guns. In fact, on March 12, Dietrich was halted about 19 miles from his starting point, but about 16 miles from his Danube objective.

The Russian riposte

On March 16, Marshals Malinovsky and Tolbukhin in their turn went over to the attack from the junction point of their two Fronts. Malinovsky planned to drive the German 6th Army back to the Danube between Esztergom and Komárom, whilst Tolbukhin, driving north-west of Lakes Velencei and Balaton,

intended to split at its base the salient made in the Soviet lines by the 6th Panzerarmee.

The 2nd Ukrainian Front's troops had the easier task and reached their first objective by March 21, cutting off four of the 6th Army's divisions.

Tolbukhin, on the other hand, met such firm resistance on March 16 and 17 from IV S.S. Panzer Corps, forming Balck's right, that the Stavka put the 6th Guards Tank Army at his disposal. However, because of Malinovsky's success, Wöhler took two Panzer divisions from the 6th Panzerarmee and set them against Malinovsky's forces. As the inequality between attack and defence became increasingly marked, Dietrich managed to

Katyushas firing in the Carpathians.

Soviet traffic during advance to Vienna, led by 2nd Ukranian Front.

evacuate the salient he had captured between March 6 and 12, and then on March 24 he brought his troops back through the bottleneck at Székesfehérvár. But what he saved from the trap was merely a hotchpotch of worn-out men with neither supplies nor equipment.

On March 27, the 6th Guards Tank Army was at Veszprém and Devecser, 35 and 48 miles from its starting point. On March 29, Tolbukhin crossed the Rába at Sárvár, and Malinovsky crossed it at Györ, where it meets the Danube. The Hungarian front had therefore collapsed; this was not surprising as Wöhler, who had no reserves, had had 11 Panzer divisions more or less destroyed between March 16 and 27.

On April 6 Hitler, consistent in his misjudgement, stripped Wöhler of command of Army Group "South" and gave it to Colonel-General Rendulic, whom he recalled from the Kurland pocket for the task.

Vienna falls

But Malinovsky had already driven between Lake Neusiedl and the Danube on April 2, and had forced the Leitha at Bruck, whilst Tolbukhin, who had captured the large industrial centre of Wiener Neustadt, launched one column along the Semmering road towards Graz and another towards Mödling and Vienna. The day he took over his command, Rendulic was informed that the advance guard of the 3rd Ukrainian Front was already in Klosterneuburg north of Vienna, and that the 2nd Ukrainian Front was already approaching it from the south. A week later, a cease-fire was signed in the famous Prater Park, but in addition to the ordeal of a week's street fighting, the wretched Viennese still had to suffer much brutality and shameless looting from their "liberators'".

Tolbukhin, who boasted of the capture of 130,000 prisoners, 1,350 tanks, and 2,250 guns, went up the right bank of the Danube, but his main forces did not go further than Amstetten, a small town 75 miles west of Vienna. On May 4, his patrols in the outskirts of Linz met a reconnaissance unit of the U.S. 3rd Army, and on the same day made contact with the advance guard of the British 8th Army on the Graz road. After helping to clear Vienna, Malinovsky sent his armies on the left across the Danube in the direction of Moravia. At Mikulov they crossed the pre-Munich (1938) Austro-Czechoslovak frontier. On the left bank of the Danube, the right wing of the 2nd Ukrainian Front, including the Rumanian 1st and 4th Armies (Generals Atanasiu and Dascalesco), liberated Slovakia and then, converging towards the north-west, occupied Brno on April 24 and were close to Olomouc when hostilities ceased. Slovakia's administration was handed over to the representatives of the Czechoslovak government-in-exile under Eduard Beneš as the occupation proceeded.

Soviet soldiers in front of Austrian parliament, Vienna, Apr 1945.

German soldiers captured in Austria by 3rd Ukranian Front, 1945.

CHRONOLOGY OF WORLD WAR II

	1938
March 11	Anschluss — German annexation of Austria.
September 29	Munich Agreement signed.
October 5	Germany occupies Sudetenland.

	1939
March 14	Slovakia declares its independence.
March 31	Britain and France give guarantee to Poland.
April 7	Italy invades Albania.
May 22	Germany and Italy sign Pact of Steel.
August 23	Molotov-Ribbentrop pact signed between Germany and the Soviet Union.
September 1	Germany invades Poland.
September 1	Britain and France declare war on Germany.
September 17	Soviet Union invades Poland.
November 30	Soviet Union at war with Finland.

	1940
March 12	War between Soviet Union and Finland ends.
April 9	Germany invades Norway and Denmark.
April 14	Allied troops land in Norway.
May 10	Fall Gelb, the offensive in the West, is launched by Germany.
May 10	Churchill becomes Prime Minister of Great Britain.
May 14	Dutch Army surrenders.
May 26	Beginning of evacuation of Dunkirk.
May 28	Belgium surrenders.
June 2	Allies withdraw from Norway.
June 4	Dunkirk evacuation complete.
June 10	Italy declares war on Britain and France.
June 14	Germans enter Paris.
June 21	Italy launches offensive against France.
June 22	France and Germany sign armistice.
June 24	France and Italy sign armistice.
July 3	Royal Navy attacks French fleet at Mers el Kebir.
July 10	Beginning of the Battle of Britain.
September 17	Operation Sealion (the invasion of England) postponed by Hitler.
September 21	Italy and Germany sign Tripartite Pact.
September 27	Japan signs Tripartite Pact.
November 20	Hungary signs Tripartite Pact.
November 22	Romania signs Tripartite Pact.
November 23	Slovakia signs Tripartite Pact.

	1941
January 19	British launch East African campaign offensive.
January 22	Australian troops take Tobruk.
February 6	British capture Benghazi.
February 11	Rommel arrives in Libya.

March 25	Yugoslavia signs Tripartite Pact.
March 27	Yugoslavia leaves Tripartite Pact after coup d'etat.
March 28	Successful British naval action against Italians off Cape Matapan.
April 6–8	Axis forces invade Yugoslavia and Greece.
April 11	U.S.A. extends its naval neutrality patrols.
April 13	Belgrade falls to Axis forces.
April 14	Yugoslav forces surrender.
April 22	Greek First Army surrenders at Metsovan Pass.
May 16	Italians surrender to British at Amba Alagi.
May 20	Germans land on Crete.
May 24	H.M.S. Hood sunk by Bismarck.
May 27	Bismarck sunk by Royal Navy.
June 1	British withdraw from Crete.
June 2	Germany launches Operation Barbarossa against the Soviet Union.
July 27	Japanese troops invade French Indo-China.
September 19	Germans capture Kiev.
September 28	Three-power Conference in Moscow.
December 6	Britain declares war on Finland, Hungary and Rumania.
December 7	Japanese attack Pearl Harbor.
December 8	U.S.A. and Britain declare war on Japan.
December 8	Japanese invade Malaya and Thailand.
December 11	Germany and Italy declare war on the U.S.A.
December 14	Japanese begin invasion of Burma.
December 25	Japanese take Hong Kong.
1942	
February 15	Japanese troops capture Singapore from British.
February 27	Battle of the Java Sea.
February 28	Japanese invade Java.
March 8	Japanese invade New Guinea.
March 17	General MacArthur appointed to command South-West Pacific.
April 9	U.S. troops surrender in Bataan.
April 16	George Cross awarded to Island of Malta by H.R.H. King George VI.
April 26	Anglo-Soviet Treaty signed.
May 6	Japanese take Corregidor.
May 7	Battle of the Coral Sea.
May 20	British troops withdraw from Burma.
May 26	Rommel's Afrika Korps attack British at Gazala.
May 30	Royal Air Force launches first thousand-bomber raid on Germany.
June 4	Battle of Midway.
June 21	Rommel's Afrika Korps take Tobruk.
July 1	Sevastopol taken by Germans.
July 1	First Battle of El Alamein.
August 7	U.S. troops land on Guadalcanal.
August 11	PEDESTAL convoy arrives in Malta.
August 19	Raid on Dieppe.

August 31	Battle of Alam Halfa.
October 24	Second Battle of El Alamein.
November 8	Operation TORCH landings in North Africa.
November 11	Germans and Italians occupy Vichy France.
November 27	French fleet scuttled at Toulon.
1943	
January 14–24	Allied Conference at Casablanca.
January 23	British troops take Tripoli.
February 2	Germans surrender at Stalingrad.
February 8	Red Army captures Kursk.
February 13	Chindits launch first operation into Burma.
February 19	Battle for the Kasserine Pass.
April 19	First Warsaw rising.
April 19	Bermuda Conference.
May 11–25	TRIDENT conference in Washington.
May 13	Axis forces surrender in North Africa.
May 16	Royal Air Force "Dambuster" raid on Mohne and Eder dams.
May 24	U-boats withdraw from North Atlantic.
July 5	Battle of Kursk.
July 10	Allies land in Sicily.
July 25	Mussolini resigns.
September 3	Allies land on Italian mainland.
September 8	Surrender of Italy announced.
September 9	Allies land at Salerno.
September 10	Germans occupy Rome and Northern Italy.
October 13	Italy declares war on Germany.
November 6	Red Army captures Kiev.
November	First Allied conference in Cairo. 23–26
November 28–December 1	Allied conference in Teheran.
December 3–7	Second Allied conference in Cairo.
December 24	General Eisenhower promoted to supreme commander for OVERLORD, the Normandy landings.
1944	
January 22	Allies land at Anzio.
January 27	Red Army raises Siege of Leningrad.
January 31	U.S. forces land on Marshall Islands.
February 1	Battle for Monte Cassino begins.
March 2	Second Chindit operation into Burma.
May 11	Fourth Battle of Monte Cassino.
June 4	U.S. troops enter Rome.
June 6	Operation OVERLORD — Allied landings in Normandy.
June 19	Battle of the Philippine Sea.
July 1	Breton Woods conference.
July 20	Failed attempt to assassinate Hitler — July Bomb plot.
August 1	Second Warsaw rising.
August 4	Allied troops enter Florence.

August 15	Operation DRAGOON — Allied landings in southern France.
August 25	Germans in Paris surrender.
September 4	British troops capture Antwerp.
September	OCTAGON — Allied conference at Quebec. 12–16
September 17	Operation MARKET GARDEN at Arnhem.
September 21	Dumbarton Oaks conference.
October 14	British enter Athens.
October 23	De Gaulle recognised by Britain and U.S.A. as head of French Provisional Government.
October 24	Battle of Leyte Gulf.
December 16	Germans launch campaign in the Ardennes.
1945	
January 4–13	Japanese Kamikaze planes sink 17 U.S. ships and damage 50 more.
January 14	Red Army advances into East Prussia.
January 17	Red Army takes Warsaw.
January 30–February 3	First ARGONAUT Allied conference at Malta.
February 4–11	Second ARGONAUT Allied conference at Malta.
February 6	Allies clear Colmar pocket.
February 19	U.S. forces land on Iwo Jima.
February 26	U.S. 9th Army reaches Rhine.
March 7	U.S. 3rd Army crosses Rhine at Remagen Bridge.
March 20	British capture Mandalay.
March 30	Red Army enters Austria.
April 1	U.S. First and Ninth Armies encircle the Ruhr.
April 1	U.S. forces land on Okinawa.
April 12	President Roosevelt dies and Truman becomes president.
April 13	Red Army takes Vienna.
April 25	U.S. and Soviet forces meet at Torgau.
April 28	Mussolini shot by partisans.
April 29	Germans sign surrender terms for troops in Italy.
April 30	Hitler commits suicide.
May 2	Red Army takes Berlin.
May 3	British enter Rangoon.
May 4	German forces in the Netherlands, northern Germany and Denmark surrender to General Montgomery on Luneburg Heath.
May 5	Germans in Norway surrender.
May 7	General Alfred Jodl signs unconditional surrender of Germany at Reims, to take effect on May 9.
May 8	Victory in Europe Day.
May 10	Red Army takes Prague.
July 17–August 2	Allied TERMINAL conference held in Potsdam.
July 26	Winston Churchill resigns after being defeated in the general election. Clement Attlee becomes Prime Minister of Great Britain.
August 6	Atomic bomb dropped on Hiroshima.
August 8	Soviet Union declares war on Japan.
August 9	Atomic bomb dropped on Nagasaki.
August 14	Unconditional surrender of Japanese forces announced by Emperor Hirohito.
August 15	Victory in Japan Day.
September 2	Japanese sign surrender aboard U.S.S. Missouri in Tokyo Bay.